GLOBAL ECONOMIC STUDIES

MEXICO, INDONESIA, SOUTH KOREA, AND TURKEY

INVESTMENT CLIMATES

Global Economic Studies

Additional books in this series can be found on Nova's website under the Series tab.

Additional E-books in this series can be found on Nova's website under the E-book tab.

GLOBAL ECONOMIC STUDIES

MEXICO, INDONESIA, SOUTH KOREA, AND TURKEY

INVESTMENT CLIMATES

ANDRES SALAZAR
EDITOR

NOVINKA

New York

For permission to use material from this book please contact us:
Telephone 631-231-7269; Fax 631-231-8175
Web Site: http://www.novapublishers.com

Additional color graphics may be available in the e-book version of this book.

LIBRARY OF CONGRESS CATALOGING-IN-PUBLICATION DATA

ISBN: 978-1-62618-863-1

Published by Nova Science Publishers, Inc. † New York

CONTENTS

Preface		**vii**
Chapter 1	2013 Investment Climate Statement: Mexico *Bureau of Economic and Business Affairs*	**1**
Chapter 2	2013 Investment Climate Statement: Indonesia *Bureau of Economic and Business Affairs*	**31**
Chapter 3	2013 Investment Climate Statement: Republic of Korea (Official Name of South Korea) *Bureau of Economic and Business Affairs*	**55**
Chapter 4	2013 Investment Climate Statement: Turkey *Bureau of Economic and Business Affairs*	**81**
Index		**109**

PREFACE

An important component of economic statecraft, investment climate statements provide U.S. firms with country-specific information and assessments prepared by posts abroad on investment laws, measures, and other factors that may be useful in making business decisions. The Investment Climate Statements help identify the barriers and market distortions that too often deter U.S. investment, provide U.S. investors with the information they need to better assess business risks, and serve as a basis for engaging foreign governments on modernizing investment regimes.

In: Mexico, Indonesia, South Korea, and Turkey ISBN: 978-1-62618-863-1
Editor: Andres Salazar

Chapter 1

2013 INVESTMENT CLIMATE STATEMENT: MEXICO*

Bureau of Economic and Business Affairs

OPENNESS TO, AND RESTRICTIONS UPON, FOREIGN INVESTMENT

Mexico is open to foreign direct investment (FDI) in most economic sectors and has consistently been one of the largest recipients of FDI among emerging markets. Mexico's macroeconomic stability and its proximity to one of the largest markets in the world have attracted investors. Mexico's new PRI government, led by President Enrique Pena Nieto, will prioritize structural economic reforms and competitiveness. The new president signed the Pact for Mexico, an agreement that details 95 priority commitments, along with the leaders of the country's three main political parties: the Institutional Revolutionary Party (PRI), the National Action Party (PAN) and the Party of the Democratic Revolution (PRD). On November 13, 2012, Mexico's legislature passed a comprehensive labor reform, which was signed into law by former President Felipe Calderon on November 29, 2012. Mexico is currently looking at expanding trade with pacific countries. On October 6,

* This is an edited, reformatted and augmented version of Bureau of Economic and Business Affairs, dated February 2013.

2012, Mexico formally joined the Trans-Pacific Partnership negotiations and in July it formed the Pacific Alliance with Peru, Colombia and Chile.

Foreign investment in Mexico has largely been concentrated in the northern states close to the U.S. border where most maquiladoras are located, and in the Federal District (Mexico City) and surrounding states, where most headquarters are located. According to the Secretariat of the Economy, Mexico is currently the top destination for aerospace manufacturing investments in the world. Financial services, automotive and electronics have received the largest amounts of FDI. Recently, Mexico's auto industry gained attention from investors as Mexico became the eighth world producer of automobiles in the world. Historically, the United States has been the main source of FDI in Mexico. In the first nine months of 2012, U.S. investors accounted for 49 percent of all FDI in Mexico.

ProMexico is the country's federal entity charged with promoting Mexican exports around the world and attracting foreign direct investment to Mexico. Through ProMexico, federal and state government efforts, as well as related private sector activities, are coordinated with the goal of harmonizing programs, strategies and resources while supporting the globalization of Mexico's economy. ProMexico maintains an extensive network of offices abroad as well as a multi-lingual website (http://www.investinmexico.com.mx which provides local information on establishing a corporation, rules of origin, labor issues, owning real estate, the maquiladora industry, and sectoral promotion plans. From 2011, ProMexico attracted 104 investment projects totaling $13.52 billion, a 27% percent increase from 2010. In the first quarter of 2012, ProMexico attracted 54 projects totaling $7 billion.

The Secretariat of the Economy also maintains a bilingual website (www.economia.gob.mx) offering an array of information, forms, links and transactions. Among other options, interested parties can download import/export permit applications, make online tax payments, and chat with online advisors who can answer specific investment and trade-related questions. State governments have also passed small business facilitation measures to make it easier to open businesses. In 2012, the Secretariat of Economy opened its International Trade Single Window to simplify import, export, and transit-related operations, increase efficiency, and reduce costs and time for international traders. The mechanism allows companies to send electronic information only once to a single entity to comply with all requirements of foreign trade. For more information on the Single Window please visit http://www.ventanillaunica.gob.mx/envucem/index.htm.

According to the most recent World Bank Study "Doing Business 2012", Mexico succeeded in easing the procedure to start a business, and improving in trading across borders, enforcing contracts, and getting electricity. Mexico moved up five positions, from 52 to 48, scoring better than Brazil, India, China and Russia. More information on the ranking can be found at: http://www.doingbusiness.org/rankings.

The 1993 Foreign Investment Law is the basic statute governing foreign investment in Mexico. The law is consistent with the foreign investment chapter of NAFTA (the North American Free Trade Agreement). It provides national (i.e. non-discriminatory) treatment for most foreign investment, eliminates performance requirements for most foreign investment projects, and liberalizes criteria for automatic approval of foreign investment. The Foreign Investment Law identifies 704 activities, 656 of which are open for 100 percent FDI stakes. There are 20 activities in which foreigners may only invest 49 percent; 13 in which Foreign Investment National Commission approval is required for a 100percent stake; five reserved only for Mexican nationals; and 10 reserved for the government of Mexico. Below is a summary of activities subject to investment restrictions:

Sectors Reserved for the State in Whole or in Part:

a) Petroleum and other hydrocarbons;
b) Basic petrochemicals;
c) Telegraphic and radio telegraphic services;
d) Radioactive materials;
e) Electric power generation, transmission, and distribution;
f) Nuclear energy;
g) Coinage and printing of money;
h) Postal service;
i) Control, supervision and surveillance of ports of entry

Sectors Reserved for Mexican Nationals:

a) Retail sales of gasoline and liquid petroleum gas;
b) Non-cable radio and television services;
c) Development Banks (law was modified in 2008);
d) Certain professional and technical services;
e) Domestic transportation for passengers, tourism and freight, except for messenger or package delivery services.

U.S. and Canadian investors generally receive national and most-favored-nation treatment in setting up operations or acquiring firms in Mexico. Exceptions exist for investments in which the Government of Mexico recorded its intent in NAFTA to restrict certain industries to Mexican nationals. U.S. and Canadian companies have the right under NAFTA to international arbitration and the right to transfer funds without restrictions. NAFTA also eliminated some barriers to investment in Mexico, such as trade balancing and domestic content requirements. Local governments must also accord national treatment to investors from NAFTA countries.

Mexico is also a party to several OECD agreements covering foreign investment, notably the Codes of Liberalization of Capital Movements and the National Treatment Instrument.

Approximately 95 percent of all foreign investment transactions do not require government approval. Foreign investments requiring applications and not exceeding USD 165 million are automatically approved, unless the proposed investment is in a sector subject to restrictions by the Mexican constitution and the Foreign Investment Law that reserve certain sectors for the state and Mexican nationals. The National Foreign Investment Commission under the Secretariat of Economy determines whether investments in restricted sectors may go forward, and has 45 working days to make a decision. Criteria for approval include employment and training considerations, technological contributions, and contributions to productivity and competitiveness. The Commission may reject applications to acquire Mexican companies for national security reasons. The Secretariat of Foreign Relations (SRE) must issue a permit for foreigners to establish or change the nature of Mexican companies.

Despite Mexico's relatively open economy, a number of key sectors in Mexico continue to be characterized by a high degree of market concentration. For example, telecommunications, electricity, television broadcasting, petroleum, beer, cement, and tortillas feature one or two or several dominant companies (some private, others public) with enough market power to restrict competition. The Mexican Congress passed some amendments to the law to strengthen the enforcement powers of the Federal Competition Commission (COFECO) in 2011, but COFECO remains weak relative to its OECD counterparts in terms of enforcement. President Pena Nieto has publicly committed his government to strengthening COFECO and to opening four key sectors (telecommunications, transportation, financial services and energy) to more competition. For more information on competition issues in Mexico please visit COFECO's bilingual website at: www.cfc.gob.mx.

Energy: The Mexican constitution reserves ownership of petroleum and other hydrocarbon reserves for the Mexican state. The energy reform package approved by the Mexican Congress in October 2008 made some progress but did not address this prohibition, and oil and gas exploration and production efforts remain under the sole purview of Pemex, Mexico's petroleum parastatal. President Pena Nieto plans to introduce a comprehensive energy reform to address these shortcomings. Many analysts believe the energy reform proposals outlined in the Pact will require constitutional amendments. While Pemex had previously contracted with foreign companies to perform specific tasks such as drilling wells, platform construction or equipment maintenance on a fee-for-service basis, the 2008 reform allowed some private participation in exploration and production of oil fields through so-called "integrated service contracts" (ISCs). In 2011, Pemex successfully completed its first bidding process for three integrated contracts for mature oil fields in Southwest Mexico. In 2012, Pemex announced its second round of ISCs. The list of companies included major oil corporations such as Chevron, Schlumberger, Halliburton and Baker Hughes. The third round of integrated service contracts is now in process, which will include the Chicontepec field. For most of the 20th century, Mexico figured among the world's largest oil producers and has been a major exporter for much of that time. Currently, however, Mexico is facing the prospect of becoming a net importer of petroleum within a decade, according to the Energy Information Agency (EIA).

The constitution also states that most electricity service may only be supplied by a state-controlled company, the Federal Electricity Commission (CFE). Earlier reforms have led to some opening to private capital. Private electric co-generation and private or municipal power projects for self-supply are now allowed; companies involved in self-supply from renewable energy sources are also permitted to generate power to be fed into CFE's grid at one location and take off the equivalent amount of power at different locations for a nominal "postage stamp" charge. Companies or households producing up to 15 kilowatts of energy are allowed to supply the excess to CFE's grid and receive credit for the energy produced. Private investors may build independent power projects, but all of their output must be sold to CFE in wholesale transactions or for self-supply. Private construction of generation for export is permitted, including generation from renewable sources of energy, particularly wind. In 1995, amendments to the Petroleum Law opened transportation, storage, marketing and distribution of natural gas imports and issued open access regulations for Pemex's natural gas transportation network.

Retail distribution of Mexico's natural gas is open to private investment, as is the secondary petrochemical industry. Pemex and CFE are also making plans to construct billions of dollars in new natural gas pipelines and are putting together tenders for financing and construction of these pipelines. In 2012, CFE awarded three pipeline contracts to U.S. companies to supply natural gas from Arizona to the western part of Mexico. Since the government's announcement in August 2001 that national and foreign private firms will be able to import liquefied petroleum gas duty-free, LNG terminals in Tamaulipas state and Baja California have begun operations, and a third facility in Manzanillo on Mexico's Pacific Coast was just completed in late 2012.

Finance Public Works Contracts (COPFs), formerly Multiple Service Contracts (MSCs) designed to comply with the country's constitution, are Mexico's most ambitious effort to attract private companies to stimulate natural gas production by developing non-associated natural gas fields. Under a COPF contract, private companies will be responsible for 100 percent of the financing of a contract and will be paid for the work performed and services rendered. However, the natural gas produced in a specific field remains the property of Pemex. Examples of work that contractors can perform include seismic processing and interpretation, geological modeling, fields engineering, production engineering, drilling, facility design and construction, facility and well maintenance, and natural gas transportation services. Some Mexican politicians still oppose COPFs as a violation of the Mexican constitution's ban on concessions. Some contracts have failed to attract any bids, demonstrating the limited success of COPFs.

Telecommunications: Mexico allows up to 49 percent FDI in companies that provide fixed telecommunications networks and services. A bill to completely open fixed telecommunications networks to foreign investors has been introduced in Congress, but the bill has been delayed several times due to a demand to include a “reciprocity clause” that would open the sector in partner countries to Mexican companies. This includes the Cable TV (CATV) industry, with one exception: companies can issue Neutral or "N" stocks up to 99 percent, which can be owned by a foreign company. In fact, one CATV company operates under this ownership scheme. There is no limit on FDI for companies providing cellular/wireless services. However, Telmex and Telcel (América Móvil) continue to reign as the dominant telecom fixed and wireless providers and wield significant influence over key regulatory and government decision makers. Mexico's dominant landline and wireless carriers are traded on the New York Stock Exchange.

Several large U.S. and international telecom companies are active in Mexico, partnering with Mexican companies or holding minority shares. Following a 2004 WTO ruling, international resellers are authorized to operate in Mexico and some companies are also looking to sell wholesale minutes to resellers. Telcel (technically independent, but majority owned by Telmex owner's Grupo Carso - Carso Global Telecom) still retains a great majority share (over 70 percent) of the cellular market. However, Spain's Telefonica Movistar, among others, continues to grow and challenge the status quo, deploying extensive mobile infrastructure to increase coverage across the country. Telmex continues to dominate the market in Long Distance (domestic and international), Internet access through DSL, and bundle services. The Convergence Accord, published in October 2006, allowed Telmex to offer broadcasting or TV services. However, the Federal Telecommunications Commission ruled that Telmex must first comply with interconnection, interoperability and number portability requirements before receiving permission to complete its triple-play offering. The accord has elicited strong concerns from the CATV industry, which fears that it will push CATV operators to consolidate. Under the accord, CATV operators (including TV duopolist Televisa's Cablevision) are allowed to independently offer Triple Play Service (VoIP-Telephony, Data-Internet and TV-Video), which might increase competition in the telephony market.

As in telecommunications, there are concerns that the two dominant television companies -- Televisa and TV Azteca, who share duopoly status in the sector -- continue to exercise influence over Mexican judicial, legislative and regulatory bodies to prevent competition. However, in August 2007 the Mexican Supreme Court ruled against the most blatant anti-competition measures of the April 2006 Radio and Television Law. Among other decisions, the Court ruled that it was unfair for broadcasting companies to keep and use at no cost analog spectrum freed from the digitalization process. The Supreme Court mandated that the Mexican Legislature draft a new media law based on its ruling. At present, U.S. firms remain unable to penetrate the Mexican television broadcast market, despite the fact that both Televisa and TV Azteca benefit from access to the U.S. market.

In 2010, the Mexican government completed the much-awaited spectrum auction of the 1.7 GHz and 1.9 GHz bands. However, a domestic wireless operator aggressively challenged the Mexican courts on the awarding of the GHz band to a U.S wireless operator. The barrage of lawsuits delayed the company's plan to expand its wireless services. However, at the end of 2011 both companies reached an out-of-court settlement.

Real Estate: Investment restrictions still prohibit foreigners from acquiring title to residential real estate in so-called "restricted zones" within 50 kilometers (approximately 30 miles) of the nation's coast and 100 kilometers (approximately 60 miles) of the borders. In all, the restricted zones total about 40 percent of Mexico's territory. Nevertheless, foreigners may acquire the effective use of residential property in the restricted zones through the establishment of a 50-year extendable trust (called a fideicomiso) arranged through a Mexican financial institution that acts as trustee.

Under a fideicomiso, the foreign investor obtains all rights of use of the property, including the right to develop, sell and transfer the property. Real estate investors should, however, be careful in performing due diligence to ensure that there are no other claimants to the property being purchased. Fideicomiso arrangements have led to legal challenges in some cases. U.S. issued title insurance is available in Mexico and a few major U.S. title insurers have begun operations here. Additionally, U.S. lending institutions have begun issuing mortgages to U.S. citizens purchasing real estate in Mexico.

Transportation: The Mexican government allows up to 49 percent foreign ownership of 50-year concessions to operate parts of the railroad system, renewable for a second 50-year period. The Mexican Foreign Investment Commission and COFECO must approve ownership above 49 percent. Consistent with NAFTA, foreign investors from the U.S. and Canada are now permitted to own up to 100 percent of local trucking and bus companies, however, several companies have encountered long wait times and legal tie-ups when trying to obtain permits.

On July 6, 2011 SCT Secretary Perez-Jacome and DOT Secretary Ray LaHood signed an MOU creating the second Long-Haul Cross-Border Trucking Program. The program is an effort to end a bilateral dispute over the free access of U.S. trucks to Mexican roads and vice versa. The first Mexican truck crossed in October of 2011 and currently six Mexican companies and a similar number of U.S. companies participate.

CINTRA, the government holding company for the Mexican airline groups, Mexicana and Aeromexico, sold Grupo Mexicana to Grupo Posadas in December 2005. Grupo Aeromexico was sold to a consortium led by Citibank-owned Banamex in October 2007. In 2010, Mexicana filed for a bankruptcy process and suspended its flights. Grupo Posada was forced to sell the airline to a new group of investors, and although there have been several interested and potential investors, the airline and the government have been so far unable to close a deal. Aeromexico obtained almost the 50% of the market since Mexicana de Aviacion suspended its operations in 2010. The emergence of low-cost domestic airlines such as Volaris and Interjet have increased competition and led to lower prices. However, foreign ownership of Mexican airlines remains capped at 25 percent and foreign ownership of airports is limited to 49 percent. Foreign express delivery service companies continue to complain that Mexican legislation unfairly favors Mexican companies by restricting the size of trucks international carriers are allowed to use.

Infrastructure: Mexican infrastructure investment, with certain previously noted exceptions, is open to foreign investment. The Mexican government has been actively seeking an increase in private involvement in infrastructure development in numerous sectors, including transport, communications, and environment. Improving Mexico's infrastructure is one of President Pena Nieto's goals during his presidency. In 2011, the Public-Private Associations Law was approved by the lower house of Congress; the law had been approved by the Senate in October 2010. The Public-Private Partnership Law allows the government to enter into infrastructure and service provision contracts with private companies for up to 40 years. The law provides more legal certainty to private investors by equally distributing risks, facilitates access to bank loans, and harmonizes existing state public-partnership models under a single federal law. National and foreign investors alike will be allowed to participate in the bidding process, except in restricted sectors as set forth by the Foreign Direct Investment law. More information on the Public-Private law can be found at: www.infraestructura.gob.mx.

Conversion and Transfer Policies

Mexico has open conversion and transfer policies as a result of its membership in NAFTA and the OECD. In general, capital and investment transactions, remittance of profits, dividends, royalties, technical service fees, and travel expenses are handled at market-determined exchange rates. Peso/dollar foreign exchange is available on same day, 24- and 48-hour settlement bases. Most large foreign exchange transactions are settled in 48 hours. The establishment of an automated clearinghouse for cross-border financial transactions between the U.S. Federal Reserve and the Bank of Mexico has facilitated payments between financial institutions in both countries. In 2010, in an effort to control money laundering activities, Mexico imposed limits on the deposit of U.S. dollars. This was extremely effective, reducing the quantity of dollars repatriated to the United States by over 50%. In a further effort to combat illicit finance, President Calderon introduced a series of laws which would establish reporting requirements for cash purchases of certain types of goods over specific monetary limits. The laws would also require "gatekeeper" professions, such as lawyers and notaries, to report on suspicious transactions. The laws have been passed by the Congress and are currently pending approval by the Senate.

EXPROPRIATION AND COMPENSATION

Under NAFTA, Mexico may not expropriate property, except for public purpose and on a non-discriminatory basis. Expropriations are governed by international law, and require rapid fair market value compensation, including accrued interest. Investors have the right to international arbitration for violations of this or any other rights included in the investment chapter of NAFTA.

There have been thirteen arbitration cases, of which six are still pending, filed against Mexico by U.S. and Canadian investors who allege expropriation, and other violations of Mexico's NAFTA obligations. Details of the cases can be found at the Department of State Website, Office of the Legal Advisor (www.state).

DISPUTE SETTLEMENT

Chapter Eleven of NAFTA contains provisions designed to protect cross-border investors and facilitate the settlement of investment disputes. For example, each NAFTA Party must accord investors from the other NAFTA Parties national treatment and may not expropriate investments of those investors except in accordance with international law.

Chapter Eleven permits an investor of one NAFTA Party to seek money damages for measures of one of the other NAFTA Parties that allegedly violate those and other provisions of Chapter Eleven. Investors may initiate arbitration against the NAFTA Party under the Arbitration Rules of the United Nations Commission on International Trade Law ("UNCITRAL Rules") or the Arbitration (Additional Facility) Rules of the International Center for Settlement of Investment Disputes ("ICSID Additional Facility Rules"). Alternatively, a NAFTA investor may choose to use the registering country's court system.

The Mexican government and courts recognize and enforce arbitral awards. The Embassy has heard of no actions taken in the Mexican courts for an alleged Chapter 11 violation on behalf of U.S. or Canadian firms. There have been numerous cases in which foreign investors, particularly in real estate transactions, have spent years dealing with Mexican courts trying to resolve their disputes. Often real estate disputes occur in popular tourist areas such as the Yucatan Peninsula. American investors should understand that under Mexican law many commercial disputes that would be treated as civil cases in the United States could also be treated as criminal proceedings in Mexico. Based upon the evidence presented, a judge may decide to issue arrest warrants. In such cases Mexican law also provides for a judicial official to issue an "amparo" (injunction) to shield defendants from arrest. U.S. investors involved in commercial disputes should therefore obtain competent Mexican legal counsel, and inform the U.S. Embassy if arrest warrants are issued.

Performance Requirements and Incentives

The 1993 Foreign Investment Law eliminated export requirements (except for maquiladora industries), capital controls, and domestic content percentages, which are prohibited under NAFTA. Foreign investors already in Mexico at the time the law became effective can apply for cancellation of prior commitments. Foreign investors who failed to apply for the revocation of existing performance requirements remained subject to them.

The Mexican federal government has eliminated direct tax incentives, with the exception of accelerated depreciation. A fiscal reform package was passed in September 2007 that includes a Flat Rate Corporate Tax (IETU). This tax limits the deductions that companies are allowed, though changes made at the behest of the business community still allow some credits for previous inventories and investments, as well as for companies that fall under the maquiladora scheme. In 2010, the IETU increased to 17.5%. Investors should follow IETU developments closely.

Most taxes in Mexico are federal; therefore, states have limited opportunity to offer tax incentives. However, Mexican states have begun competing aggressively with each other for investments, and most have development programs for attracting industry. These include reduced price (or even free) real estate, employee training programs, and reductions of the 2% state payroll tax, as well as real estate, land transfer, and deed registration taxes, and even new infrastructure, such as roads. Four northern states --Nuevo

Leon, Coahuila, Chihuahua and Tamaulipas -- have signed an agreement with the state of Texas to facilitate regional economic development and integration. Investors should consult the Finance, Economy, and Environment Secretariats, as well as state development agencies, for more information on fiscal incentives. Tax attorneys and industrial real estate firms can also be good sources of information. U.S. Consulates have reported that the states in their consular districts have had to modify their incentive packages due to government decentralization. Many states have also developed unique industrial development policies.

Mexico's maquiladora industry is governed by the Ministry of Economy's, IMMEX program. Please refer to the Ministry of Economy's IMMEX program website at http://www.economia.gob.mx/?P=immex for more information. Companies interested in investing in industrial activity in Mexico need to follow the new IMMEX guidelines closely, preferably in close consultation with locally based legal advisors. The Mexican government's recent modifications to the industry's tax regime provide companies with financial and operational benefits, such as development of Mexico's maquila-servicing and supply industries. Other modifications to the IMMEX Program include: reducing the grounds for which the government can terminate a company's inclusion in the IMMEX Program (and exempts certain qualified companies from being excluded at all); eliminates the requirement that companies submit certain information to both the Secretariat of Economy and the Mexican Tax Service (companies will now only be required to submit the information one time); and extends the temporary importation term for raw materials from 18 months to 36 months for certified companies (or 60 months for companies registered in the Inventory Control System, SECIIT).

In order to maintain competitiveness of maquiladora companies and comply with NAFTA provisions, Mexico has developed "Sectoral Promotion Programs" (PROSEC). Under these programs, most favored nation import duties on listed inputs and components used to produce specific products are eliminated or reduced to a competitive level. These programs comply with NAFTA provisions because import duty reduction is available to all producers, whether the final product is sold domestically or is exported to a NAFTA country. PROSECs supported 24 sectors, including electronic and home appliances, automotive, and auto parts, textile, and apparel, footwear and others. However, since 2008, the government has eliminated some tariffs included in the PROSECs that have not been used for several years or that already have a most favored nation low import duty thanks to a new trade policy implemented by the government. The reduction of PROSECs concluded in 2012. In December 2008, former President Felipe Calderon issued in the Official Gazette (Diario Oficial) an immediate and gradual reduction of import duties for more than 10,000 tariffs in order for companies to obtain inputs at competitive prices.

When the gradual elimination and reduction of import duties concludes in 2013, the tariff structure will have six basic rates: 0, 5%, 7%, 10%, 15% and 20%. On December 26, 2011 a decree was issued to eliminate 230 tariffs included in 21 of the 24 PROSECs since they already have an equal or higher most favored nation import duty. (http://www.economia.gob.mx/?P=944).

Right to Private Ownership and Establishment

Foreign and domestic private entities are permitted to establish and own business enterprises and engage in all forms of remunerative activity in Mexico, except those mentioned in Section One.

Private enterprises are able to freely establish, acquire and dispose of interests in business enterprises. The two most common types of business entities are corporations (Sociedad Anonima) and limited partnerships (Sociedad de Responsibilidad Limitada).

Under these legal entities a foreign company may operate an independent company, a branch, affiliate, or subsidiary company in Mexico.

The rules and regulations for starting an enterprise differ for each structure.

To form a corporation (Sociedad Anonima), the rules are:

a. Can be up to 100 percent foreign-owned;
b. Must have a minimum of 50,000 Mexican pesos in capital stock to start;
c. Must have minimum of two shareholders, with no maximum. Board of Directors can run the administration of the company;
d. The enterprise has an indefinite life span;
e. Free transferability of stock ownership is permitted;
f. Operational losses incurred by the Mexican entity or subsidiary may not be used by the U.S. parent company;
g. Limited liability to shareholders.

To form a Limited Liability Company (Sociedad de Responsabilidad Limitada), the rules are:

a. Can be up to 100 percent foreign-owned;
b. Must have a minimum of 3,000 Mexican pesos in capital stock to start;
c. Must have a minimum of two partners to incorporate a corporation with limited liability. The partners must manage the company but 50 is the maximum number of shareholders;
d. Exists only when the business purpose and partners remain the same;
e. Restricted transferability of partnership shares. Any changes in the partnership composition may cause the partnership to be liquidated;
f. If structured properly, it may offer tax advantages by allowing operational losses incurred by the Mexican entity to be used by the U.S. parent company;
g. Limited liability is afforded the partners.

Protection of Intellectual Property Rights

Two different laws provide the core legal basis for protection of intellectual property rights (IPR) in Mexico -- the Industrial Property Law (Ley de Propiedad Industrial) and the Federal Copyright Law (Ley Federal del Derecho de Autor). Multiple federal agencies are responsible for various aspects of IPR protection in Mexico. The Office of the Attorney General (Procuraduría General de la Republica, or PGR) has a specialized unit that pursues criminal IPR investigations. The Mexican Institute of Industrial Property (Instituto Mexicano de la Propiedad Industrial, or IMPI) administers Mexico's trademark and patent registries and is responsible for handling administrative cases of IPR infringement. The National Institute of Author Rights (Instituto Nacional del Derecho de Autor) administers Mexico's copyright register and also provides legal advice and mediation services to copyright owners who believe their rights have been infringed. The Mexican Customs Service (Aduanas México) plays a key role in ensuring that illegal goods do not cross Mexico's borders.

Despite strengthened enforcement efforts by Mexico's federal authorities over the past several years, weak penalties and other obstacles to effective IPR protection have failed to deter the rampant piracy and counterfeiting found throughout the country. The U.S. Government continues to work with its

Mexican counterparts to improve the business climate for owners of intellectual property.

Mexico is a signatory to at least sixteen international treaties that deal with IPR, including the Paris Convention for the Protection of Industrial Property, the NAFTA, and the WTO Agreement on Trade-related Aspects of Intellectual Property Rights. Though Mexico signed the Patent Cooperation Treaty in Geneva, Switzerland in 1994, which allows for simplified patent registration procedure when applying for patents in more than one country at the same time, it is necessary to register any patent or trademark in Mexico in order to claim an exclusive right to any given product. A prior registration in the United States does not guarantee its exclusivity and proper use in Mexico, but serves merely as support for the authenticity of any claim you might make, should you take legal action in Mexico. Mexico signed the Anti-Counterfeit Trade Agreement (ACTA) on July 12, 2012. It is still pending ratification by the Mexican congress.

Although a firm or individual may apply directly, most foreign firms hire local law firms specializing in intellectual property. The U.S. Embassy's Commercial Section maintains a list of such law firms in Mexico at: http://export.gov/mexico/businessserviceproviders/index.asp

Transparency of Regulatory System

The Federal Commission on Regulatory Improvement (COFEMER), within the Secretariat of Economy, is the agency responsible for reducing the regulatory burden on business. The Mexican government has been making steady progress on this issue in the last few years. On a quarterly basis, these agencies must report to the President on progress achieved toward reducing the regulatory burden. In December 2006, President Calderon replaced the Regulatory Moratorium Agreement, issued by the previous administration, to ensure agencies streamline their regulatory promulgation processes, with the Quality Regulatory Agreement. The new agreement intends to allow the creation of new regulations only when agencies prove that they are needed because of an emergency, the need to comply with international commitments, or obligations established by law.

The federal law on administrative procedures has been a significant investment policy accomplishment. The law requires all regulatory agencies to prepare an impact statement for new regulations, which must include detailed information on the problem being addressed, the proposed solutions, the alternatives considered, and the quantitative and qualitative costs and benefits and any changes in the amount of paperwork businesses would face if a proposed regulation is to be implemented.

The Mexican government, with the OECD, the private sector and several think tanks, has worked to streamline bureaucracy and procedures, with a particular focus on several Mexican states. Thanks to this effort, Mexico improved its ranking in the 2013 World Bank Doing Business Report going from 53 in 2012 to 48. Mexico made significant improvements in business registration and registration of new firms, such as the elimination of the requirement to have minimum capital to create a new business and the creation of a collateral registry. Although Mexico still needs to approve some legal reforms to make this registry stronger, it was a step in the right direction to unify information on collateral under some sort of centralized registry. Despite these measures, many difficulties remain. Foreign firms continue to list bureaucracy, slow government decision-making, lack of transparency, and a heavy tax burden among the principal negative factors inhibiting investment in Mexico, particularly in states and municipalities. However, the OECD and the new administration will continue working to improve the regulatory process at the subnational level. The Secretariat of Public Administration, which will disappear under the Pena administration to make room to a new National Anti-Corruption Agency, made considerable strides in improving transparency in government, including government contracting and involvement of the private sector in enhancing transparency and fighting corruption. The Mexican government has established several Internet sites to increase transparency of government processes and establish guidelines for the conduct of government officials. "Normateca" provides information on government regulations; "Compranet" allows for on-line federal government procurement; "Tramitanet" permits electronic processing of transactions within the bureaucracy thereby reducing the chances for bribes; and "Declaranet" allows for online filing of income taxes for federal employees.

Efficient Capital Markets and Portfolio Investment

The Mexican banking sector has strengthened considerably since the 1994 Peso Crisis left it virtually insolvent. Since the crisis, Mexico has introduced reforms to buttress the banking system and to consolidate financial stability.

These reforms include creating a more favorable economic and regulatory environment to foster banking sector growth by reforming bankruptcy and lending laws, moving pension fund administration to the private sector, and raising the maximum foreign bank participation allowance. The bankruptcy and lending reforms passed by Congress in 2000 and 2003 effectively made it easier for creditors to collect debts in cases of insolvency by creating Mexico's first effective legal framework for the granting of collateral. Pension reform allows employees to choose their own pension plan. Allowing banks or their holding companies to manage these funds provides additional capital to the banking sector, while the increased competition permits fund managers to focus on investment returns. In December 2007, the Mexican Congress approved amendments to the Law of Credit Institutions (LIC) that included creating a new limited banking license and transferring power from the Mexican tax authority to the Banking and Securities Commission (CNBV), the primary banking regulator.

The financial profile of the banking sector has improved due to the reduction in the problem assets brought about by write-offs, problem loan sales, and the conclusion of most debt-relief programs. These developments, combined with more stringent capital requirements, have contributed to an improvement in the level and composition of capital across the banking system, particularly among the larger institutions. The banking sector remains highly concentrated, with a handful of large banks controlling a significant market share, and the remainder comprised of regional players and niche banks. The Mexican Tax Authority has approved the opening of several new banks since 2006, including Wal-Mart Bank and Prudential Bank, but the sector's competitive dynamics and credit quality are still being driven by six large banks (Banamex, Bancomer, Santander, HSBC, Banorte and Scotiabank)—five of which are foreign-owned. The newcomers are mostly focused on the unbanked population and will present only limited competition to the group of old banks. Bank lending, especially consumer lending and mortgages, grew rapidly in 2005 and 2006, fueled by lower interest rates and historically low inflation. However, the global financial crisis slowed down all types of lending in 2008 and 2009. According to the CNBV, total loan balances rose to 2.358 trillion pesos ($172 billion dollars) at the end of October 2011, a 13% increase from 2010. Businesses and consumers are demanding more credit as the economy enjoys an export-led rebound, with 2011 posting gross domestic product (GDP) growth of 3.9%. Economists widely expect an expansion of 3.9% for 2012. The Mexican Bank Association has forecast further double digit loan growth this year.

Small- and medium-sized businesses still complain of a lack of access to credit, but government-owned development banks have begun to expand their lending to this sector. Despite the expansion, such lending remains low 1 % of GDP, compared to 28% in Brazil. Private banks argue that due diligence in lending to such business is difficult given the large amount of revenue they keep off the books to avoid increased tax liability. This position may reflect the healthy profits the banks earn from existing business models, currently more than 8% return on assets compared to 2.5% in the United States.

Commercial loans to established companies with well-documented accounts are available in Mexico, but many large companies utilize retained earnings to fund growth. Supplier credit is the main source of financing for many businesses. The largest companies are able to issue debt for their financing needs on domestic markets, tapping into a growing pool of pension funds looking for investment options. Non-bank financing is generally available, however, to large companies with strong credit ratings and important commercial ties with their suppliers -- i.e., companies that could easily procure bank financing. The Secretariat of Finance and Public Credit sets regulatory policy and oversees the CNBV. Mexico's central bank, the Bank of Mexico (Banxico), also has a regulatory role in addition to setting monetary policy. The Institute for the Protection of Bank Savings (IPAB) handles deposit insurance for up to 400,000 Mexican pesos.

Reforms creating better regulation and supervision of financial intermediaries and fostering greater competition have helped strengthen the financial sector and capital markets. These reforms, coupled with sound macroeconomic fundamentals, have created a positive environment for the financial sector and capital markets, which have responded accordingly. The implementation of NAFTA opened the Mexican financial services market to U.S. and Canadian firms. Foreign institutions hold more than 70 percent of banking assets and banking institutions from the U.S. and Canada have a strong market presence. Under NAFTA's national treatment guarantee, U.S. securities firms and investment funds, acting through local subsidiaries, have the right to engage in the full range of activities permitted in Mexico.

Foreign entities may freely invest in government securities. The Foreign Investment Law establishes, as a general rule, that foreign investors may hold 100 percent of the capital stock of any Mexican corporation or partnership, except in those few areas expressly subject to limitations under that law. Regarding restricted activities, foreign investors may also purchase non-voting shares through mutual funds, trusts, offshore funds, and American Depositary Receipts. They also have the right to buy directly limited or nonvoting shares as well as free subscription shares, or "B" shares, which carry voting rights. Foreigners may purchase an interest in "A" shares, which are normally reserved for Mexican citizens, through a neutral fund operated by a Mexican Development Bank. Finally, state and local governments, and other entities such as water district authorities, now issue peso-denominated bonds to finance infrastructure projects. These securities are rated by international credit rating agencies. This market is growing rapidly and represents an emerging opportunity for U.S. investors.

Competition from State Owned Enterprises

The Mexican Constitution constrains private investment in the hydrocarbon sector. Articles 27 and 28 specifically establish the monopoly control of the State. Mexico's energy sector faces one of the most restrictive regimes in the world. During the past 15 years, there have been changes in the law to allow some private investment in electric co-generation and self-supply, as well as power generation for export, and, as part of the 2008 energy reform, to permit companies to enter into "performance-linked" contracts for hydrocarbon exploration and drilling. Amendments to the Petroleum Law opened transportation, storage, marketing and distribution of natural gas imports and issued open access regulations for Pemex's natural gas transportation network, as well as retail distribution of Mexico's natural gas and secondary petrochemical industry. Since 2001, the government allowed national and foreign private firms to import liquefied petroleum gas duty-free.

There are two main state-owned companies in the energy sector. Mexican Petroleum (Pemex) is in charge of running the hydrocarbons (oil and gas) sector, which includes upstream, mid-stream, and downstream operations, and is the most important fiscal contributor to the country. In 2011 and 2012, Pemex contributed 34% to the Mexican government's budget, but current declines in productivity will have major consequences for the Mexican government as Pemex is Mexico's largest taxpayer. The Federal Electricity Commission (CFE) is the other main state-owned company and is in charge of the electricity sector. As required by the Constitution, the electricity sector is also federally owned, with CFE controlling most of installed generating capacity. CFE also holds a monopoly on electricity transmission and distribution. It operates Mexico's national transmission grid, which consists of 27,000 miles of high voltage lines, 28,000 miles of medium voltage lines, and 370,000 miles of low voltage distribution lines. It generates electric power for almost 33.8 million customers (or 100 million people). The infrastructure to generate electric power is made up of 177 generating plants, having an installed capacity of 51,081 megawatts. Reforms to the electricity sector now permit independent power producers to develop projects and sell their electricity to CFE, and for CFE to solicit bids from private companies for new power plant construction: 22.41% of CFE's current installed capacity stems from 21 plants which were built using private capital by Productores Independientes de Energía (PIE). Attempts to reform the sector, including the subsidized rates provided to agricultural users and some consumers, have traditionally faced strong political and social resistance in Mexico, even though the existence of subsidies for residential consumers absorbs substantial fiscal resources.

The President of the United Mexican States appoints the Director General or Chief Executive Officer (CEO) of PEMEX. The Mexican Government closely regulates and supervises the operations of PEMEX through three Ministries and one Commission: The Secretary of Energy (Sener) monitors the company's activities, and serves as the chairman of Pemex's Board of Directors; the National Hydrocarbons Commission (CNH), which is independent but report to Sener's Secretary of Energy, evaluates Pemex's reserve estimates and provides regulations for Pemex's operations in all areas, including deep-water exploration and drilling and gas flaring; the Secretary of Finance and Public Credit (SHCP) reviews and incorporates the annual budget and financing program of Pemex and its subsidiaries; and the Secretary of Environment and Natural Resources (Semarnat), in coordination with other federal and state authorities, regulates Pemex's activities that affect the environment.

Pemex has a board of directors, which includes government representatives from the Secretary of Energy, Secretary of Finance, the Secretary of Public Function, and the Office of the President; four professional members; five representatives from the union; one commissioner; and one independent auditor, which in this case is the private consulting group, KPMG. Pemex's accounting and balance sheets are subject to internal and external audits. The Audit and Performance Evaluation Committee of PEMEX's Board of Directors appoints PEMEX's external auditors. Pemex's financial reports are issued in accordance with Mexico's Generally Accepted Accounting Principles (GAAP), which differ somewhat from U.S. GAAP. PEMEX has registered bond issuances in the Securities and Exchange Commission (SEC). Thus, in order to maintain its registration with the SEC, PEMEX has the obligation to file several international standard forms, such as the Form 20-F, on an annual basis. Pemex has also issued bonds in the domestic market, and in accordance with the Stock Market Law, it also has to submit audited quarterly and annual reports to the National Banking and Securities Commission. These reports, along with the annual Hydrocarbons Reserves Report and the Primary and Financial Balance, are published on Pemex's webpage. The state-owned oil company has moved forward in incorporating best corporate and social responsibility practices.

The CFE is a decentralized government agency, duly incorporated, and controls its own assets. Like Pemex, CFE has a Board of Directors, which includes representatives from the Secretariats of Energy, Environment, Social Development, Economy, Finance; Pemex's CEO; and three representatives from the union. CFE's books are also subject to domestic general accounting rules and are reviewed by independent auditors. The Energy and Finance Secretariats approve and submit Pemex's and CFE's budgets to the lower house for approval.

The Servicio Postal Mexicano (Sepomex), or Correos de Mexico, is the national postal service of Mexico and officially retains a monopoly on all mail items under one kilogram. The mail is regulated under Mexico's Communications and Transport Secretariat, and postal service is reserved to the state under Mexico's Constitution. Private delivery under one kilogram is officially illegal, but loopholes in the law have allowed some domestic and foreign privately-owned shippers to provide some delivery services through certified delivery and other advanced-service options to differentiate their business from that of a standard postal delivery. In the past, there were calls for legal reforms that would give Correos de Mexico a strictly enforced monopoly on packages weighing 350 grams or less and require private couriers to charge up to seven times Correos de Mexico's prices, but the government has not moved ahead on this front.

Technically, Correos de Mexico is responsible for financing itself, but the government does subsidize the agency if there is insufficient revenue. Liberalization and privatization of postal markets are not currently on the agenda in Mexico. Correos de Mexico has a Board of Directors presided over by the Ministry of Communications and Transportation. Other members of the Board are: the Secretary of Foreign Affairs, the Secretary of the Economy, the Secretary of Finance, and the Under Secretary of Communications. The Director General is appointed by the President.

CORPORATE SOCIAL RESPONSIBILITY

Both the private and public sector have taken several actions to promote and develop Corporate Social Responsibility (CSR) in Mexico during the past decade. CSR in Mexico began more as a philanthropic effort, but it has gradually evolved to a more holistic approach, trying to match international standards, such as the OECD Guidelines for Multinational Enterprises and the United Nations Global Compact. The Mexican Center of Philanthropy (CEMEFI), a well-respected NGO for the promotion of CSR and philanthropy, was created in 1998, and among its achievements has been the creation of the CSR distinctive award in 2001 to those companies that comply with CSR best practices in Mexico and Latin America. Other awards that recognize companies' CSR work in Mexico are the Great Place to Work rank and Expansion magazine's Super Empresas list. Some of the domestic and foreign companies, of the more than one hundred that have received awards, are: Bimbo, Nestlé, Coca Cola, WalMart, Hewlett Packard, General Electric, Pfizer, and many more.

In 2005, the Mexican Standards Institute (IMNC) officially issued the CSR standard NMX-SAST-004-IMNC. On November 26, 2010, Mexico officially launched the ISO 26000 Guidance on Social Responsibility, an international standard that offers guidance on socially responsible behavior and possible actions; it does not contain requirements and, therefore, in contrast to ISO management system standards, is not certifiable. Corporate social responsibility reporting has made progress in the last few years with more companies developing a corporate responsibility performance strategy. The government has also made an effort to implement CSR in state-owned companies such as PEMEX, which has published corporate responsibility reports since 1999.

POLITICAL VIOLENCE

Peaceful mass demonstrations are common in the larger metropolitan areas such as Mexico City, Guadalajara, and Monterrey. While political violence is rare, narcotics- and organized-crime-related violence has skyrocketed since 2006. Transnational criminal organizations (TCOs) fighting each other and the government for control of drug smuggling routes have carried out violent acts unprecedented both in number and nature. 2012 saw more than 12,000 organized crime-related homicides, a similar level as 2011, according to widely cited press reports. Cartels use torture and the public dumping of bodies to intimidate their rivals. As the Mexican government increases the pressure, TCOs continue to expand their operations into any available money-making venture, including kidnappings, extortion, human trafficking, and hijacking cargo shipments, often targeting business owners and others innocent of any involvement in narcotics trafficking.

The United States is working with Mexico to combat organized crime and enhance rule of law through the Merida Initiative. This initiative is a three year-old program to provide equipment and training to support law enforcement operations and technical assistance for long-term reform and oversight of security agencies, as well as to build a 21stcentury border and help rebuild communities torn apart by violence. So far the U.S. Congress has appropriated over $1.5 billion USD for this initiative, which has provided, among other things, helicopters and surveillance aircraft, non-intrusive inspection equipment, technical assistance, and training to strengthen investigative techniques, prison systems, border management, and judicial practices. In addition, the Merida Initiative has supported Mexican investments in job creation programs, engaging youth in their communities, expanding social safety nets, and building community confidence in public institutions to create a culture of lawfulness and undercut the allure of the cartels. Though the violence is not political in nature, U.S. Embassy Mexico notes that general security concerns remain an issue for companies looking to invest in the country. Many companies choose to take extra precautions for the protection of their executives. They also report increasing security costs for shipments of goods. The Overseas Security Advisory Council (OSAC) monitors and reports on regional security for American businesses operating overseas. OSAC constituency is available to any American-owned, not-for-profit organization, or any enterprise incorporated in the U.S. (parent company, not subsidiaries or divisions) doing business overseas (https://www.osac.gov/). The Department of State maintains a Travel Warning for U.S. citizens traveling and living in Mexico, available at: http://travel.state.gov/travel /cis_pa_tw/tw/tw_5665.html

CORRUPTION

Corruption is pervasive in almost all levels of Mexican government and society. President Calderon pledged that his government would fight against corruption in government agencies at the federal, state and municipal levels. Aggressive investigations and operations have exposed corruption at the highest levels of government. President Pena Nieto through PRI lawmakers submitted to the Mexican congress proposals to reorganize his cabinet, among which is the creation of a National Anti-Corruption Commission, which will absorb the duties of the present Secretariat of Public Function/Administration, which currently has the government's anti-corruption oversight role. The aim is to have an impartial and autonomous entity with full capacity to combat corruption.

Former president Felipe Calderon signed into law the Federal Anti-corruption law in June 2012 and the anti-money laundering law (or the illicit finance law) in October 2012. The anti-money laundering law obligates Designated Non-Financial Businesses & Professions (DNFBP) to identify their clients and report suspicious operations or transact ions about designated thresholds to the Secretariat of Finance (SHCP), establishes a Specialized Financial Analysis Unit (UEAF) in the Office of the Attorney General (PGR), restricts cash operations in Mexican pesos, foreign currencies and precious metals for a variety of "vulnerable" activities, and imposes criminal sanctions and administrative fines on violators of the new legislation. For more information on the anti-money laundering law, please consult http://www.dof.gob.mx/nota_detalle.php?codigo=5273403&fecha=17/10/2012

Mexico ratified the OECD Convention on Combating Bribery in May 1999. The Mexican Congress passed legislation implementing the convention that same month. The legislation includes provisions making it a criminal offense to bribe foreign officials. Mexico is also a party to the OAS Convention against Corruption and has signed and ratified the United Nations Convention against Corruption. The government has enacted or proposed strict laws attacking corruption and bribery, with average penalties of five to ten years in prison. The Transparency and Access to Public Government Information Act, the country's first freedom of information act, went into effect in June 2003 with the aim of increasing government accountability. Mexico's 31 states have passed similar freedom of information legislation that mirrors the federal law and meets international standards in this field. Transparency in public administration at the federal level has noticeably improved, but access to information at the state and local level has been slow.

According to Transparency International's 2012 Index of Corruption Perception, Mexico scored 3.4 on a scale of 1 to 10 where lower numbers represent a greater perception of corruption. The tally places Mexico in 105th place out of 176 nations, a drop from 100th place 9out of 183 nations) in 2011.

Local civil society organizations focused on fighting corruption are still developing in Mexico. A handful of Mexican non-governmental organizations, including Mexico Without Corruption and the FUNDAR Center for Analysis and Investigation, work to study issues related to corruption and raise awareness in favor of transparency. The Mexican branch of Transparency International also operates in Mexico. The best source of Mexican government information on anti-corruption initiatives is the Ministry of Public Administration (www.funcionpublica.gob.mx).

Bilateral Investment Agreements

NAFTA governs U.S. and Canadian investment in Mexico. In addition to NAFTA, most of Mexico's eleven other free trade agreements (FTAs) cover investment protection, with a notable exception being the Mexico-European Union FTA. The network of Mexico's FTAs containing investment clauses include Bolivia, Chile, Costa Rica, Colombia, El Salvador, Guatemala, Honduras, Japan, and Nicaragua. A Free Trade Agreement with Peru and also a combined agreement with Central America passed Mexico's Congress in December 2011.

Mexico has enacted formal bilateral investment protection agreements with 27 countries: 15 European Union countries (Austria-Belgium, Luxembourg, Denmark, Finland, France, Germany, Greece, Italy, Netherlands, Portugal, Spain, Sweden, United Kingdom and the Czech Republic), as well as Australia, Argentina, Belarus, China, Cuba, Iceland, India, Panama, Slovakia, South Korea, Switzerland, Trinidad and Tobago, and Uruguay. Mexico continues to negotiate bilateral investment treaties with Russia, Saudi Arabia, Malaysia, Singapore, Brazil and the Dominican Republic.

The United States and Mexico have a bilateral tax treaty to avoid double taxation and prevent tax evasion. Important provisions of the treaty establish ceilings for Mexican withholding taxes on interest payments and U.S. withholding taxes on dividend payments. The implementation of the flat tax on January 1, 2008 has led to questions as to whether the new tax meets the requirements of the bilateral tax treaty. The U.S. Internal Revenue Service presently allows businesses to credit flat tax against their U.S. taxes and has stated that it will issue a ruling at some future date. Businesses should continue to monitor this issue.

Mexico and the United States also have a tax information exchange agreement to assist the two countries in enforcing their tax laws. The Financial

Information Exchange Agreement (FIEA) was enacted in 1995, pursuant to the Mutual Legal Assistance Treaty. The agreements cover information that may affect the determination, assessment, and collection of taxes, and investigation and prosecution of tax crimes. The FIEA permits the exchange of information with respect to large-value or suspicious currency transactions to combat illegal activities, particularly money laundering. Mexico is a member of the financial action task force (FATF) of the OECD and has made progress in strengthening its financial system through specific anti-money-laundering legislation enacted in 2000 and 2004. In 2010, Mexico implemented restrictions on U.S. dollar deposits which reduced by 50% the amount of bulk cash repatriated to the United States from the Mexican financial system. However, Mexico needs to approve the proposed Law for the Prevention of Illicit Finance Operations, pending in Congress, to limit peso cash purchases, give the Attorney General's office sole jurisdiction over the investigation and prosecution of money laundering cases, and to oblige more economic agents, such as notaries, consultants, and attorneys to report suspicious operations.

OPIC and Other Investment Insurance Programs

In August of 2004, Mexico and the U.S. Overseas Private Investment Corporation (OPIC) finalized an agreement that enables OPIC to offer all its programs and services in the country. Since then, OPIC has pursued potential investment projects in Mexico, and the country rapidly became one of the top destinations for projects with OPIC support. OPIC is actively providing over $730 million in financing and political risk insurance support to 17 projects in Mexico. In addition, OPIC-supported funds are among the largest providers of private equity capital to emerging markets. OPIC's current active projects in Mexico are worth $681 million. For more information on OPIC's projects in Mexico, please consult OPIC's website at www.opic.gov.

Labor

After months of negotiations in the Mexican Congress, former President Felipe Calderon signed a sweeping labor reform bill into law on November 29, 2012. The new law encompasses major changes to make Mexico's labor market flexible and incorporate modern statutes such as non-discrimination.

Included in the 300 articles are provisions for the easing of hiring-and-firing of workings, establishing an apprenticeship system, establishing an hourly wage system, and regulating outsourcing. The labor reform also prohibits job discrimination based on sex, health, sexual preference, age, and disability. It makes it illegal for employers to require pregnancy tests of their female workers and job candidates. The new law also makes it a federal offense to employ children under the age of 14. The reform also restructures Mexico's labor courts and incorporates the International Labor Organization's (ILO) concept of decent work. The full text of the new law can be found at http://www.stps.gob.mx/bp/micrositios/reforma_laboral/ref_lab.html.

There is a large surplus of labor in the formal economy, largely composed of low-skilled or unskilled workers. On the other hand, there is a shortage of technically skilled workers and engineers. Labor-management relations are uneven, depending upon the unions holding contracts and the industry concerned. Many actors also note that the Mexican government wields veto power in the supposedly neutral and balanced tripartite arrangement of labor-business relations. Mexican manufacturing operations in the textile and garment sectors are experiencing stiff wage competition from Central America and India, but gaining relative wage competition with China in high technology sectors. Mexico's minimum wage averages around US$5 per day and is less than a living wage in this OECD country. It is set by the tripartite National Commission for Minimum Wage each year.

FOREIGN TRADE ZONES/FREE PORTS

In addition to the IMMEX programs that operate as quasi-free trade zones, in 2002 Mexico approved the operation of more traditional free trade zones (FTZ). Unlike the previous "bonded" areas that only allowed for warehousing of product for short periods, the new FTZ regime allows for manufacturing, repair, distribution, and sale of merchandise. There is no export requirement for companies operating within the zone to avail themselves of tax benefits. Regulatory guidance for FTZs can be found under Mexico's Customs Law, article 14 D. Most major ports in Mexico have bonded areas ("recinto fiscalizados") or customs agents ("recintos fiscal") within them. Mexico currently has four approved FTZ's, located in San Luis Potosi, Mexico City, Monterrey, and Guanajuato.

Foreign Direct Investment Statistics Source: Mexico's Secretariat of Economy

Foreign Direct Investment in Mexico (USD Million)

	2008	2009	2010	2011	3Q2012
Total FDI Inflow	26564.9	15829.2	19792.1	20823.3	13045.1
New Investments	11567.7	7103.8	12995.4	12298.8	4547.3
Earnings Reinvestment	7518.6	4247.1	2656.6	6960.3	4713.5
Inter-company Investment	7861.7	4224.3	3974.6	1564.2	3784.3

Foreign Direct Investment Realized in Mexico by Industrial Sector Destination (USD Million)

	2008	2009	2010	2011	3Q2012
Total FDI Inflow	26564.9	15829.2	19792.1	20823.3	13045.1
Extractive	4734.1	725.6	933.2	976.6	467.9
Manufacturing	7898.6	5519.2	11318.2	9628.3	5070.8
Electricity and Water	460.8	60.6	4.2	-218.8	126.3
Construction	1350.7	702.8	122	1673.5	1230.9
Transportation	381.3	101.1	159	285.2	205.1
Financial Services	4154.8	2445.7	1796.3	2470	1930.2

Foreign Direct Investment Inflows Realized By Country/Economy of Origin (USD Million)

	2008	2009	2010	2011	3Q2012	5 Year totals
Total FDI	26564.9	15829.2	19792.1	20823.3	13045.1	96054.6
United States	11038	7178	5356	10618	6403	40593
Spain	4882	2677	1450	332.7	212.3	9554
France	197.4	239.6	112.6	204	335	1088.6
United Kingdom	1288.4	345.5	520	641	402.3	3197.2
Canada	3055.4	1608.8	1134.7	750.6	589	7138.5
Switzerland	224.3	82.3	234.8	1157.7	145.9	1845
Germany	608.5	37.1	306.7	376.8	713.6	2042.7
Japan	142.4	221.4	225	766	676.2	2031

The chart summerizing well-regarded indexes and rankings (MCC refers to the Millennium Challenge Corporation)

Measure	Year	Index/Ranking
TI Corruption Index	2012	105
Heritage Economic Freedom	2013	67
World Bank Doing Business	2012	48
MCC Govt. Effectiveness	2011	64
MCC Rule of Law	2011	38.97
MCC Control of Corruption	2011	45
MCC Regulatory Quality	2011	61

In: Mexico, Indonesia, South Korea, and Turkey ISBN: 978-1-62618-863-1
Editor: Andres Salazar

Chapter 2

2013 INVESTMENT CLIMATE STATEMENT: INDONESIA*

Bureau of Economic and Business Affairs

OPENNESS TO, AND RESTRICTIONS UPON, FOREIGN INVESTMENT

Indonesia's growing middle class, strong domestic demand, stable political situation, and conservative macroeconomic policy paired with gross domestic product (GDP) growth of 6.5% in 2011 make Indonesia an attractive destination for Foreign Direct Investment (FDI). In 2012, Indonesian government officials welcomed increased FDI, aiming to create jobs and spur economic growth, and courted foreign investors, notably focusing on participation in a large number of public private partnerships to develop Indonesia's infrastructure. However, vague and conflicting regulations, poor existing infrastructure, rigid labor laws, and corruption continued to be significant concerns for foreign investors. U.S. firms lamented the lack of ministerial coordination but were encouraged with apparent increased accessibility to the Indonesian parliament (DPR) in 2012.

Restrictions on FDI are, for the most part, outlined in presidential decree 36/2010, commonly referred to as the Negative List. The Negative List consolidates FDI restrictions from numerous decrees and regulations to create

* This is an edited, reformatted and augmented version of Bureau of Economic and Business Affairs, dated March 2013.

greater certainty for foreign and domestic investors. The 2010 iteration of the Negative List, the most recent version, clarified that companies are grandfathered-in in the case of increased foreign ownership restrictions. However, exceptions remain; in the case of wholly foreign owned security service companies, their licenses were not renewed, despite grandfathering provisions. In 2010, the share of foreign ownership permitted was increased in health services, creative industries, construction services, and multilevel marketing, but decreased in cell towers, security services, and inspection services. For investment in certain sectors, such as mining and higher education, the Negative List is useful only as a starting point, as additional licenses and permits are required from individual ministries. Foreign capital investment, through the stock market, is not governed by the Negative List. Foreigners may purchase equity in state-owned firms through initial public offerings. Capital investments in publicly listed companies through the stock exchange are not subject to Indonesia's Negative List unless an investor is buying a controlling interest.

The Investment Coordinating Board (BKPM) is responsible for issuing investment licenses to foreign entities and has taken steps to simplify the application process through better coordination between various government institutions. In 2012, BKPM launched the online portal for its National Single Window for Investment which allows foreign investors to apply for and track the status of licenses and other services online. Although BKPM is meant to act as a one-stop service institution, investments in the mining, oil and gas, plantation, and other sectors require further licenses from related ministries and authorities.

Likewise, certain tax and land permits, among others, typically must be obtained from local government authorities. Though Indonesian companies only require one approval at the local level, businesses report that foreign companies often must obtain both administrative and *de facto* legislative approval in order to establish a business.

The Coordinating Ministry of Home Affairs, Ministry of Administrative Reform and Bureaucracy Reform, and BKPM issued a circulating letter on September 15, 2010, to clarify investment that crosses provincial and regional boundaries. Investment in one regency is managed by the regency government; investment that lies in two or more regencies is managed by the provincial government; and investment that lies in two or more provinces is managed by central government, or central BKPM.

Natural Resources

Indonesia's vast natural resource wealth has attracted significant foreign investment over the last century, and remains one of the most prospective countries in the world. But a variety of government regulations have made doing business in the resources sector increasingly difficult, and Indonesia now ranks in the bottom 10% among the world's 90+ mining countries in the Fraser Institute's mining Policy Potential Index. In 2012 the Government of Indonesia (GOI) banned the export of raw minerals, dramatically increased the divestment requirements for foreign mining companies, and required major mining companies to renegotiate their contracts of work with the government. The 2009 mining law devolved mining license issuing authority to local governments, who have responded by issuing more than 10,000 licenses, many of which overlap or are unclearly mapped. In the oil and gas sector, Indonesia's Constitutional Court disbanded the upstream regulator, injecting confusion and more uncertainty into the natural resources sector.

Measure	Year	Index/Ranking
TI Corruption Index	2012	32/118 of 176
Heritage Economic Freedom	2012	56.4/115 of 179
World Bank Doing Business	2012	128 of 185
MCC Government Effectiveness	2013	0.20 (66%)
MCC Rule of Law	2013	-0.19 (34%)
MCC Control of Corruption	2013	-0.16 (28%)
MCC Fiscal Policy	2013	-1.3 (83%)
MCC Trade Policy	2013	75.0 (48%)
MCC Regulatory Quality	2013	0.02 (56%)
MCC Business Start Up	2013	0.927 (41%)
MCC Land Rights Access	2013	0.67 (43%)
MCC Natural Resource Protection	2013	99.8 (94%)
MCC Access to Credit	2013	29 (49%)
MCC Inflation	2013	5.4 (59%)

Infrastructure

Indonesia's Master Plan for Acceleration and Economic Development (MP3EI), launched in 2011, is an ambitious 15-year, $1 trillion infrastructure development plan that includes several public-private partnership tenders and will require almost $700 billion in private financing. Though the MP3EI is a positive development, implementation has been lacking and project groundbreakings a year after its launch represented just 10% of the total plan's projected value.

Conversion and Transfer Policies

The rupiah (Rp), the local currency, is freely convertible. Currently, banks must report all foreign exchange transactions and foreign obligations to the Bank of Indonesia (BI).

With respect to the physical movement of currency, any person taking cash into or out of Indonesia in the amount of Rp 100 million ($11,000) or more, or the equivalent in another currency, must report the amount to the Director General of Customs and Excise.

Banks on their own behalf or for customers may conduct derivative transactions related to derivatives of foreign currency rates, interest rates, and/or a combination thereof.

BI requires borrowers to conduct their foreign currency borrowing through domestic banks registered with BI. The regulations apply to borrowing in cash, non-revolving loan agreements, and debt securities.

Under the 2007 Investment Law, the GOI gives assurance to investors relating to the transfer and repatriation of funds, in foreign currency, on capital, profit, interest, dividend and other income, funds required for (i) purchasing raw material, intermediate goods or final goods, and (ii) replacing capital goods for continuation of business operations, additional funds required for investment project, funds for debt payment, royalties, income of foreign individual working on the invested project, earnings from selling or liquidation of invested company, compensation for losses, and compensation for expropriation. U.S. firms report no difficulties in obtaining foreign exchange.

Bank Indonesia began in 2012 to require exporters to repatriate their export earnings through domestic banks within three months of the date of the export declaration form.

Once repatriated, there are currently no restrictions on re-transferring export earnings abroad. Some companies report this requirement is not fully enforced.

EXPROPRIATION AND COMPENSATION

The GOI generally recognizes and upholds property rights of foreign and domestic investors, and the 2007 Investment Law opened major sectors of the economy to foreign investment while assuring investors' protection from nationalization, except where corporate crime is involved.

While there have been no overt expropriatory actions forced on investors in recent years, Indonesia's rising resource nationalism and ensuing action in the mining sector has raised concern about the Government's willingness to protect and fairly compensate foreign miners' property rights going forward. Mining companies that hold still-valid contracts of work with the central government are required to renegotiate the terms of those contracts, including higher tax and royalty rates, as well as divestment of equity to Indonesian interests. In 2012, the GOI issued a regulation requiring foreign-owned mining operations to divest majority equity to Indonesian shareholders within 10 years of operational startup. It appears the GOI plans to use cost of investment incurred, rather than market value, for purposes of divestment valuation.

A requirement to refine all ore domestically before it can be exported is another GOI priority advanced under the 2009 Mining Law that could lead to depressed domestic ore prices if enforced. In general, Indonesia's rising resource nationalism supports the idea that domestic interests should not have to pay prevailing market prices for domestic resource interests. The domestic market obligation on oil and gas producers is a longstanding example of this expectation. New investors in Indonesia's mining sector no longer have the security of a long-term contract of work with the central government, but are instead issued mining licenses by the local regent, whose term of office is five years. The security of the mining license, and what compensation the local regent is prepared to offer (if any) in the case of its cancellation, is uncertain.

The Law on Land Acquisition Procedures for Public Interest Development passed in December 2011 seeks to streamline GOI acquisition of land for much-needed infrastructure projects. The law seeks to clarify roles, impose time limits on each phase of the land acquisition process, deter land speculation, and curtail obstructionist litigation, while still ensuring safeguards for land-right holders. However, because the crucial power of revoking land rights rests with provincial governors, the new law's effectiveness – or potential misuse as a tool of expropriation – will depend in part on the inclination of respective governors.

Dispute Settlement

Indonesia's legal system is based on civil law. The court system consists of District Courts (primary courts of original jurisdiction), High Courts (courts of appeal), and the Supreme Court (the court of last resort). Indonesia also has a Constitutional Court. The Constitutional Court has the same legal standing as the Supreme Court, and its role is to review the constitutionality of legislation. Both the Supreme and Constitutional Courts have authority to conduct judicial review.

Judicial handling of investment disputes remains mixed. Indonesia is a signatory to the Convention On The Settlement Of Investment Disputes Between States And Nationals Of Other States (ICSID) and the New York Convention of 1958 on the Recognition and Enforcement of Foreign Arbitral Awards. Thus, foreign arbitral awards are legally recognized and enforceable in the Indonesian courts, but, in practice, are not always enforced. Indonesia's legal code recognizes the right of parties to apply any rules of arbitration upon which they mutually agree. Some arbitration but not all is handled by Indonesia's domestic arbitration agency, the Indonesian National Arbitration Body. District Courts do not have authority to hear disputes where parties are bound by an arbitration agreement. In reality, some claims are still accepted by District Courts on the basis of tort or fraud, but are often reversed upon appeal. Some companies have resorted to ad hoc arbitrations in Indonesia using the UN Commission on International Trade Laws (UNCITRAL) arbitration rules. In 2012, U.S. cotton exporters saw an increase in cotton contract defaults by Indonesian companies. Though doing business in Indonesia remains challenging, there is not a clear pattern of investment disputes involving U.S. or other foreign investors.

The court system often does not provide effective recourse for resolving property and contractual disputes. Judges are not bound by precedent and many laws are open to various interpretations. A lack of clear land titles has plagued Indonesia for decades, although the land acquisition law enacted in December 2011 included legal mechanisms that may begin to resolve some past land ownership issues. Indonesia also has a poor track record on contract sanctity. Government Regulation 79 of 2010 opened the door for the GOI to remove recoverable costs from production sharing contracts. The GOI is also requiring mining companies to renegotiate their contracts of work to require higher royalties, more divestment, more local content, and domestic processing of mineral ore. Indonesia's commercial code, grounded in colonial Dutch law, has been updated to include provisions on bankruptcy, intellectual property rights, incorporation and dissolution of businesses, banking, and capital markets. Application of the commercial code, including the bankruptcy provisions, remains uneven, in large part due to corruption and training deficits for judges, prosecutors, and defense lawyers. The bankruptcy law is decidedly pro-creditor and the law makes no distinction between domestic and foreign creditors. As a result, foreign creditors have the same rights as all potential creditors in a bankruptcy case, as long as foreign claims are submitted in compliance with underlying regulations and procedures. Monetary judgments in Indonesia are made in local currency.

Performance Requirements/Incentives

The Indonesian government notified the WTO of its compliance with Trade-Related Investment Measures (TRIMS) on August 26, 1998. The 2007 Investment Law states that the GOI shall provide the same treatment to both domestic and foreign investors originating from any country pursuant to the rules of law.

In 2011, the GOI announced a tax holiday scheme to exempt certain businesses from paying corporate income taxes for up to ten years under Ministry of Finance Decree No. 130/PMK.011/2011. Businesses must have operated as a legal entity in Indonesia for at least 12 months prior to the issue of the tax holiday regulation, among other requirements. Priority is given to investment in resource extraction, resource refinement, industrial machinery, renewable resources, telecommunications equipment, or pioneer sectors. Government Regulation No. 62 of 2008 provides a tax incentive program for projects conducted in national high-priority sectors which encompass 128 different fields. Businesses may only apply for one tax incentive: either the tax holiday or the tax incentive program.

The GOI expects foreign investors to contribute to the training and development of Indonesian nationals, allowing the transfer of skills and technology required for their effective participation in the management of foreign companies. As a general rule, a company can hire foreigners only for positions that the government has deemed open to non-Indonesians. Employers must have manpower-training programs aimed at replacing foreign workers with Indonesians. If a direct investment enterprise wants to employ foreigners, the enterprise should submit an Expatriate Placement Plan to BKPM to get a Limited Stay Visa or Semi Permanent Residence Visa (VITAS/VBS). Expatriates are issued a Limited Stay Permit (KITAS) and a blue book, valid for two years and renewable for up to two extensions without leaving the country. Under Ministry of Manpower regulations, any expatriate who holds a work and residence permit must contribute $1,200 per year to a fund for local manpower training at regional manpower offices. Some U.S. firms report difficulty in renewing KITASs for their foreign executives.

With the passage of the 2012 defense law in October, the GOI plans to impose offset or local content requirements for procurements from foreign defense suppliers. Currently, U.S. defense equipment suppliers are still competing for contracts with local partners on the basis of an exception in the law that indicates that purchases may be made from non-state owned enterprise (SOE) sources if not readily available on the local market. Further clarification through additional regulation will reveal how rigid the application of the new requirements will be.

The GOI grants special preferences to encourage domestic sourcing and to maximize the use of local content in government procurement. It also instructs government departments, institutes, and corporations to utilize domestic goods and services to the maximum extent feasible. The Negative List seeks to maximize local content in procurement, use foreign components only when necessary, and delegate foreign contractors as sub-contractors to local companies. Foreign firms bidding on high value government sponsored projects report that they have been asked to purchase and export the equivalent value of selected Indonesian products if they are awarded the contract. Some businesses established as Indonesian entities report discrimination as they possess higher foreign equity.

The Ministry of Law and Human Rights' implementation of an electronic business registration filing and notification system has dramatically reduced the number of days needed to register a company. Foreign firms are not required to disclose proprietary information to the government before investing.

At present, Indonesia does not have formal regulations granting national treatment to U.S. and other foreign firms participating in Government-financed or subsidized research and development programs. The State Ministry for Research and Technology handles applications on a case-by-case basis.

Exporters to Indonesia must comply with numerous and overlapping import licensing requirements that impede access to Indonesia's market. In 2012, Indonesia issued new regulations overseeing the importation of finished products. In recent years, the Government implemented sweeping regulation imposing non-automatic import licensing procedures on a broad range of products, including horticultural and livestock products, electronics, household appliances, textiles and footwear, toys, and food and beverage products. This regulation also includes a requirement for pre-shipment verification by designated surveyors at importers' expense and a restriction that limits entry of imports to five designated ports and airports.

In July 2012, Indonesia added to the list of goods prohibited for export. Some of the goods forbidden for export include: natural rubber, rattan and certain types of wood, some live fish, giant tiger prawns, natural sand, precious stones, and antiques.

Indonesia's average most favored nation applied tariff was 7% in 2011. Over the past several years, Indonesia has raised tariffs on a number of products. In August 2012, Indonesia raised tariffs on most metal and mineral ores (but not coal) to 20%. Indonesia also imposes a 40% tariff on unprocessed palm fruit and 20% on oil cake and tiered tariffs for crude palm oil and other oil palm derivatives. In December 2012, the Indonesian government also issued a 20% emergency safeguard tariff on wheat flour imports for 200 days. In August 2012, Indonesia temporarily removed a 5% soybean import tax through the end of 2012. In 2010, Indonesia increased applied tariffs for products including medicines, cosmetics, and energy efficient lights. Most Indonesian tariffs are bound at 40%, although bound tariff levels exceed 40% or remain "unbound" on automobiles, iron, steel, and some chemical products.

Right to Private Ownership and Establishment

Indonesia recognizes the right to private ownership and establishment by both foreign and domestic entities. Foreign investors are restricted from establishing or acquiring businesses in certain sectors as laid out in the Negative List. Private entities have the right to dispose of interests in business enterprises under Indonesia's bankruptcy law, although it may take several years to do so. Likewise, terminating employees is associated with high costs and a lengthy process that requires bipartite negotiation, non-binding mediation, and Labor Court approval unless settled by agreement in writing at any time during the process.

To establish a business, one must: obtain the standard form of the company deed; arrange for a notary electronically; obtain clearance for the Indonesian company's name at the Ministry of Law and Human Rights; notarize company documents; obtain a certificate of company domicile from the local municipality; pay the State Treasury for the non-tax state revenue fees for legal services; apply to the Ministry of Law and Human Rights for approval of the deed of establishment; apply at the one stop service for the permanent business trading license and company registration certificate; register with the Ministry of Manpower; apply for the workers social security program; and, obtain a taxpayer registration number and a valued added tax (VAT) collector number. The process takes an average of 47 days.

PROTECTION OF PROPERTY RIGHTS

The Basic Agrarian Law of 1960, the predominant body of law governing land rights, recognizes the right of private ownership. Indonesia's 1945 Constitution states that all natural resources are owned by the GOI for the benefit of the people. This principle was augmented by the passage of a land acquisition bill in December 2011 that enshrined the concept of eminent domain and established mechanisms for fair market value compensation and appeals. The National Land Agency registers property under Regulation No. 24 of 1997, though the Ministry of Forestry administers all 'forest land'. Registration is sometimes complicated by local government requirements and claims as a result of decentralization. Registration is also not conclusive evidence of ownership, but rather strong evidence of such. Foreigners are not allowed to own land in Indonesia, but can acquire the rights to use, sell, lease, and mortgage land through an Indonesian entity. The Ministry of Housing has proposed foreign ownership rights for properties in the special economic zones of Batam, Bintan, and Karimun. However, these plans have been delayed due to an ongoing revision of the Agrarian Law.

Indonesia is currently on the Special 301 priority watch list for intellectual property rights (IPR) protection. Indonesia's failure to effectively protect intellectual property and enforce IPR laws has resulted in high levels of physical and online piracy. The International Intellectual Property Alliance estimates that 86% of business software is unlicensed, while retail piracy rates are likely even higher.

Indonesia's 2002 Copyright Law and 2001 Trademark Law are currently under review. While not fully adequate, both laws provide a solid foundation for enforcement efforts. However, enforcement has been insufficient. The Copyright Law requires commercial courts to try cases of alleged copyright violations and render judgments within 90 days, though it often takes much longer. Even so, criminal cases against corporate end-user piracy in Jakarta and Semarang have been successfully prosecuted.

The GOI has signed and ratified the WIPO internet treaties, but further clarifications in its Copyright Law must be made to fully implement both treaties.

Transparency of the Regulatory System

Indonesia continues to bring its legal, regulatory, and accounting systems into compliance with international norms, but progress is slow. Recent successes include passage of a comprehensive anti-money laundering law in late 2010 and a land acquisition law in December 2011, both of which have positive implications for foreign investment.

Although Indonesia continues to move forward with regulatory system reforms, these efforts have not yet created a level playing field for foreign investors nor does the current regulatory system establish clear and transparent rules for all actors. Certain laws and policies, including the Negative List, establish sectors that are either fully off-limits to foreign investors or are subject to substantive conditions.

A proposed revision to Indonesia's 2003 labor law may establish more stringent restrictions on outsourcing, currently used by many firms to circumvent some formal-sector job benefits that tend to make the labor market rigid and uninviting to potential investors. Bureaucratic reforms have slowed, and decentralization has introduced another layer of bureaucracy for firms to navigate, resulting in costly red tape. Ineffective management and corruption are among the challenges faced by the GOI in launching bureaucratic reform. U.S. businesses cite regulatory and transparency problems as ongoing factors hindering operations.

Government ministries and agencies, including the Indonesian Parliament, continue to publish many proposed laws and regulations in draft form for public comment; however, not all draft laws and regulations are made available in public fora.

Laws and regulations are often vague and require substantial interpretation by the implementers, leading to business uncertainty and rent-seeking opportunities. In short, investors remain interested but wary, as Indonesia is not currently making the longer-term regulatory changes to generate substantive domestic or foreign investment.

EFFICIENT CAPITAL MARKETS AND PORTFOLIO INVESTMENT

Although there is some concern regarding the operations of the many small, family-owned banks, the banking system is generally considered sound with banks enjoying some of the widest interest rate margins in the region. The ten largest banks, with Rp 2,472 trillion ($256.6 billion) in total assets or 61.7% of the total, dominate the banking sector. Loans grew 23.0% year-on-year as of October 31, 2012, (vis-à-vis 26.0% in 2011) while gross non-performing loans stood at 2.3%, down from 3.0% a year earlier.

Foreigners may purchase up to 99% of the total shares of a domestic bank through private placement or on the stock exchange. Purchases of 25% or more require BI approval. Foreign banks may establish branches if the foreign bank is ranked in the top 200 global banks by assets. To establish a representative office, the foreign bank must be ranked in the top 300 global banks by assets. A special operating license is required from BI in order to establish a foreign branch.

BI is considering limiting bank ownership to no more than 50% by any single shareholder, applicable to foreign and domestic shareholders, and requiring foreign bank branches to become subsidiaries.

The Indonesia Stock Exchange (IDX) index closed at 4,316.69 on December 28, 2012, up 12.9% for the calendar year. As of December 28, 2012, IDX had 454 listed companies with a total capitalization Rp 4,126.99 trillion ($428.3 billion). There were 23 initial public offerings in 2012. Foreigners conducted about 43.0% of the total stock trades in 2012. In 2011, the IDX launched the Indonesian Sharia Stock Index (ISSI), its first index of sharia-compliant companies, primarily to attract greater investment from Middle East companies and investors. The ISSI is composed of 214 stocks that are already listed on IDX's Jakarta Composite Index.

Government treasury bonds are the most liquid bonds offered by the GOI. Treasury bills are less liquid due to their small issue size. Liquidity in BI-issued Sertifikat Bank Indonesia (SBI) is also limited due to the six-month required holding period. As of December 2012, the government's total gross bond sales (including international bond issuance) had reached Rp 820.7 trillion ($85.2 billion). The GOI also issued its first sukuk treasury bills as part of efforts to diversify Islamic debt instruments and increase their liquidity. Indonesia's sovereign debt was upgraded to investment grade by Fitch Ratings in December 2011 and by Moody's in January 2012.

The corporate bond market is dominated by banks and automotive financing companies. Trading in the corporate bond market by value was up 17.0% as of December 28, 2012. For the twelve month period ending December 28, 2012, total outstanding corporate bonds rose 27.0% to Rp 189.4 trillion ($19.7 billion).

The Financial Services Supervisory Authority (OJK) will assume BI's supervisory role over commercial banks as of January 1, 2014. OJK will also oversee the capital markets and non-banking institutions as of January 1, 2013, replacing the Capital Market and Financial Institution Supervisory Board.

Foreigners have good access to the Indonesian securities market and are a major source (29.7% in government securities) of portfolio investment. Foreign ownership of Indonesian companies may be limited in certain industries as determined by the Negative List.

Competition from State-Owned Enterprises (SOEs)

Indonesia has 141 SOEs, 26 of which contributed more than 90% of the total SOE profit. Sixteen are listed on the Indonesian stock exchange and 14 are special purpose entities such as the Indonesian Infrastructure Guarantee Fund. SOEs are present in almost every sector including banking, tourism, agriculture, forestry, mining, construction, fishing, energy, and telecommunications. In 2012, the profits of SOE rose by 11% to Rp 128 trillion ($13.3 billion) compared to 2011. SOEs employ around 780,000 people and contribute an estimated 40% of the country's gross domestic product. Currently, SOEs command around 53% of market share in the cellular telecommunication sector in terms of number of subscribers, hold around 37% of the banking sector's total assets, 52% of the cement sector's total sales, and 50% of the total energy supply.

GOI has stated it will consolidate the number of SOEs in order to increase efficiency and benefits. The consolidation is expected to take place through mergers, privatization, establishing sectoral holding companies, or liquidation. The government expects the number of SOEs to decrease to 78 in 2014 to 25 in 2025.

Private enterprises can compete with SOEs under the same terms and conditions with respect to access to markets, credit, and other business operations. However, some sectors reported that, in reality, SOEs receive increased preference for GOI projects. SOEs publish an annual report and are audited by the Supreme Audit Agency (BPK), the Financial and Development Supervisory Agency (BPKP), and external and internal auditors.

Indonesian SOEs adopt a two-tier Board structure with a Board of Commissioners (similar to an American company's board of directors) and a Board of Directors (similar to an American company's executive management team).

Depending on the type of SOE, either the President or the Minister of SOEs has the right to make appointments and to dismiss members of either the Board of Commissioners or Board of Directors. With such control, board member appointments are subject to government interference. Hence, it is not uncommon for SOEs to have ministers, high-ranking bureaucrats, military generals, or member of political parties, either retired or still active, sitting as Board members. Some SOEs suffer from poor management, which has led to several cases of graft and corruption against former Commissioners and Directors.

The GOI established the Pusat Investasi Pemerintah (PIP) to act as a special purpose investment entity and eventually as a sovereign wealth fund. To date, it has limited its investments to the domestic market in strategic sectors with the goal of stimulating national economic growth. PIP can invest in a variety of asset classes such as equity, debt, infrastructure, and direct investments.

PIP is in addition to other GOI SOEs that invest in domestic markets such as PT Sarana Multi Infrastructure, PT Indonesia Infrastructure Guarantee Facility, and Indonesia Infrastructure Finance.

Corporate Social Responsibility (CSR)

While international organizations like the OECD and UN envision CSR as a comprehensive management paradigm that includes concepts like human rights, employee relations, environment and science, bribery and corruption, consumer interests, and taxation, understanding of CSR in Indonesia tends to focus on community and economic development, and educational projects and programs.

This is at least in part caused by the fact that such projects are often required in the environmental impact permits ("Amdal") of resource extraction companies, who undergo a good deal of domestic and international scrutiny of their operations. Because much resource extraction activity occurs in remote and rural areas where government services are limited or absent, these companies face very high community expectations to provide such services themselves. Despite significant investments – especially by large multinational firms – in CSR projects, there is limited general awareness of those projects, even among government regulators and officials.

Political Violence

As in other democracies, politically motivated demonstrations occur regularly throughout Indonesia. Such demonstrations on occasion become violent, but are not a major ongoing concern for most foreign investors. Public reaction to events in the Middle East, including anti-U.S. demonstrations, continues to be limited to sporadic protests, mostly nonviolent.

Fighting terrorism remains a top priority for the Indonesian government, and President Yudhoyono has demonstrated a continued strong commitment to combating terrorism. Since the 2009 bombings of two international hotels in Jakarta, Indonesian police and security forces have disrupted a number of terrorist cells, including some affiliated with Jemaah Islamiyah (JI), a U.S. government-designated terrorist organization that carried out several bombings at various times since 2000.

In response to terrorist threats and attacks, Indonesia has effectively pursued counterterrorism efforts through legislation and law enforcement. In 2012, the Attorney General's Office handled nearly 50 terrorism related case. Violent elements in Indonesia continue to demonstrate a willingness and ability to carry out attacks with little or no warning. Although U.S. and Western-affiliated interests remain potential targets of terrorists, the focus of terrorists is increasingly on attacks against local governments and law enforcement entities, especially the police.

Foreign investors in Papua face certain unique challenges relative to those operating in other parts of Indonesia. Indonesian security forces are engaged in operations against the Free Papua Movement, a small armed separatist group. Low-intensity communal, tribal, and political conflict also exists in Papua and has caused deaths and injuries. Anti-government protests have resulted in deaths and injuries. Between 2009 and 2012, gunfire from unknown attackers on the private roads from Timika to Tembagapura caused several casualties, including deaths, of government security forces, local workers, and one expatriate.

Corruption

President Yudhoyono campaigned and was re-elected in 2009 on a strong anti-corruption platform. However, corruption remains a serious problem, preventing increased FDI, according to some U.S. companies. Although the government has issued detailed directions on combating corruption in targeted ministries and agencies, there has not been a concerted government-led effort to encourage or require companies to establish internal codes of conduct, or effective internal controls, ethics, and compliance programs to detect and prevent bribery of public officials.

Indonesia's ranking in Transparency International's Corruption Perceptions Index in 2012 is 118 out of 183 countries. Corruption remains pervasive despite laws to combat corruption and a strong, independent Corruption Eradication Commission (KPK). The KPK's purview in corruption cases is typically limited to law enforcement and other public officials, cases that exceed $105,000 in value and/or that represent significant loss to the state. Corruption cases are also handled by the Indonesian National Police and Attorney General's Office, neither of which have the same organizational capacity to investigate or prosecute corruption cases. Giving or accepting a bribe is a criminal act, with possible fines ranging from $5,500 to $110,000 and imprisonment up to a maximum of 20 years, depending on the severity of the charge.

Indonesia ratified the UN Convention Against Corruption in September 2006. Indonesia has not yet acceded to the OECD Anti-Bribery Convention, but attends meetings of the OECD Anti-Corruption Working Group. Indonesia is a co-chair along with the United Kingdom of the Open Government Partnership, a multilateral platform to promote transparency, empower citizens, fight corruption, and strengthen governance. Several civil society organizations function as vocal and competent corruption watchdogs, including Transparency International Indonesia and Indonesia Corruption Watch.

Bilateral Investment Agreements

Indonesia has signed investment protection agreements with 60 countries, including: Algeria, Argentina, Australia, Bangladesh, Belgium, Bulgaria, Cambodia, Chile, Croatia, Cuba, Czech Republic, Denmark, Egypt, Finland,

France, Germany, Hungary, India, Iran, Italy, Jamaica, Jordan, Kyrgyzstan, Laos, Malaysia, Mauritius, Mongolia, Morocco, Mozambique, North Korea, Norway, Pakistan, People's Republic of China, Peru, Philippines, Poland, Qatar, Romania, Saudi Arabia, Singapore, Slovak Republic, South Korea, Spain, Sri Lanka, Sudan, Suriname, Syria, Sweden, Switzerland, Thailand, The Netherlands, Tunisia, Turkey, Turkmenistan, Ukraine, United Kingdom, Uzbekistan, Vietnam, Yemen, and Zimbabwe.

Indonesia has extensive preferential trade relationships with other Asian countries. Under the ASEAN Free Trade Agreement (FTA), import duties from ASEAN countries are applied at 0% to 5%, except for products specified on an exclusion list. In addition, Indonesia accords preferential market access to Australia, China, Japan, Korea, India, and New Zealand (under ASEAN FTAs) and to Japan and Pakistan (under bilateral agreements). Implementation of the ASEAN-China FTA has been contentious, with domestic industries pressing for more time to implement tariff commitments as well as for the imposition of new non-tariff barriers to offset the reduction in tariff protection. Indonesia is currently negotiating bilateral agreements with Iran, India, Australia, New Zealand, and European Free Trade Association countries, and undertaking studies on potential FTAs with Chile, Turkey, South Korea, Tunisia, Mexico, South Africa, and Egypt.

Non double income taxation between the United States and Indonesia is granted in accordance with the Convention between the Government of the Republic of Indonesia and the Government of the United States of America for the Avoidance of Double Taxation and the Prevention of the Fiscal Evasion with Respect to Taxes on Income, signed at Jakarta July 11, 1988, and its amending Protocol, signed at Jakarta July 24, 1996.

OPIC and Other Investment Insurance Programs

In 2010, the Overseas Private Investment Corporation (OPIC) updated its 1967 investment support agreement between the United States and Indonesia by adding OPIC products such as direct loans, coinsurance, and reinsurance to the means of OPIC support which U.S. companies may use to invest in Indonesia.

Indonesia has joined the Multilateral Investment Guarantee Agency (MIGA). MIGA, a part of the World Bank Group, is an investment guarantee agency to insure investors and lenders against losses relating to currency transfer restrictions, expropriation, war and civil disturbance, and breach of contract. The Indonesian Rupiah may be purchased using the exchange rate provided by BI pursuant to the current rate on the date of the transaction. The BI exchange rate can be found at www.bi.go.id. In 2012, the Rupiah depreciated 6% against the USD.

LABOR

Labor became a prominent issue for foreign investors in 2012 due to significant increases in the minimum wage for many provinces, including a 44% increase in Jakarta, and significant restrictions on the use of contract workers. Indonesian labor is relatively low cost by world standards, but the country's education system and rigid labor laws combine to make Indonesia's competitiveness lag behind other Asian competitors. Investors frequently cite high severance payments to dismissed employees, restrictions on outsourcing and contract workers, and limitations on expatriate workers as significant obstacles to new investment in Indonesia. Lack of education is especially problematic among unskilled and semi-skilled workers. Labor contracts are relatively straightforward to negotiate but are subject to renegotiation, despite the existence of written agreements. Local courts are prone to side with local citizens in labor disputes, contracts notwithstanding. On the other hand, some foreign investors view Indonesia’s labor regulatory framework, respect for freedom of association, and the right unionize as an advantage to investing in the country. The GOI established in January 2006 a new Labor Court as part of a broader labor dispute resolution system. U.S. companies expressed disappointment in the GOI’s lack of mediation between labor groups and industry during 2012 minimum wage discussions. Expert local human resources advice is essential for American companies doing business in Indonesia, even those only opening representative offices. Indonesia's highly fractured and largely ineffective labor movement has gained strength in recent years, evidenced by significant increases in the minimum wage. Minimum wages vary throughout the country as provincial governors set an annual minimum wage floor and district heads have the authority to set a higher rate. Many provinces are expected to see large increases in 2013. The governor of Jakarta has agreed to a 2013 minimum wage of $232, a 44% increase over 2012 and an increase of 97 % since 2010. In October 2011, the Indonesian government passed a revised Social Security Law to take effect in January 2014 that will establish a national agency to support workers in the event of work accident, death, retirement, or old age.

Foreign Trade Zones/Free Ports

The GOI offers incentives to over 1,500 foreign and domestic industrial companies that operate in bonded zones throughout Indonesia. The largest bonded zone is the free trade zone island of Batam, located just south of Singapore. Investors in bonded zones are not required to apply for additional implementation licenses (location, construction, and nuisance act permits and land titles), and foreign companies are allowed 100% ownership. These companies do not pay import duty, income tax, VAT, and sales tax on imported capital goods, equipment, and raw materials until the portion of production destined for the domestic market is "exported" to Indonesia, in which case fees are owed only on that portion. Companies operating in bonded zones may lend machinery and equipment to subcontractors located outside of the bonded zone for a maximum two-year period. A recent Ministry of Finance Regulation No. 147/2011 stipulates that the delivery of products outside of bonded zones into the domestic market is set at a maximum of 25% (down from 50%) of export realization value of the previous year. If a bonded zone company exceeds the 25% limitation, its domestic quota for the next year will be reduced. The new regulation also restricts subcontract work and requires bonded zones less than 10,000 square meters in size to relocate to industrial estates. As stipulated by the 2007 Investment Law, the Indonesian Legislature (DPR) passed regulations on special economic zones (SEZ) in 2009. At least 20 areas have submitted applications for SEZ status, but only two were created in 2012: Sei Mangke in North Sumatra and Tanjung Lesung in Banten.

Foreign Direct Investment Statistics

Indonesia has two main sources for FDI statistics: BKPM, which issues permanent business licenses to domestic and foreign investors, and BI, which records international capital flows as part of balance of payments statistics. BKPM records FDI figures based on issued business licenses. Since licenses for oil and gas, mining, banking, non-bank financial institutions, insurance and leasing are issued by other government bodies, these sectors are not covered under the BKPM statistics. BKPM is expected to increase the sectoral coverage gradually while BI statistics cover all sectors. BKPM categorizes all investments made into a foreign capital investment company as FDI, even if it is a joint venture with a local partner. This practice tends to inflate BKPM's FDI figures, which may additionally include equity contributions from domestic partners and investments financed from domestic sources. BI instead follows the standard FDI categorization of equity investment, retained earnings and other capital inflows.

Table 1. FDI by industry in USD million

	2005	2006	2007	2008	2009	2010	2011
Agriculture & Forestry	3	225	286	197	-52	286	284
Fishing	9	4	19	-25	10	52	61
Mining & Quarrying	1,226	322	1,904	3,610	1,302	1,896	3,882
Manufacturing	5,264	1,691	2,412	2,322	1,573	4,971	8,157
Electricity, Gas and Water	162	-1	-61	-56	53	204	364
Construction	130	85	195	24	7	-49	411
Wholesale & Retail	60	375	215	1,159	73	2,463	2,882
Hotel & Restaurant	0	7	-10	16	0	1	-1
Transport, Storage & Communication	384	592	919	134	1,799	2,389	2,378
Financial Intermediation	780	1,027	1,361	1,927	149	408	559
Real Estate and Business Activity	17	-14	-4	-201	-25	27	687
Others	0	599	37	212	-11	654	-353
TOTAL	8,338	4,914	6,928	9,318	4,876	13,303	19,242
% of GDP	2.9	1.3	1.6	1.8	0.9	1.9	2.2

Note: Public Administration & Defense, Education, Health, Other Community Services all recorded zero FDI.

Source: Bank Indonesia.

Table 2. FDI by Country of Origin in USD million

	2005	**2006**	**2007**	**2008**	**2009**	**2010**	**2011**
Japan	1,542	1,057	1,126	1,144	896	3,728	5,194
U.S.	3,442	-549	1,093	1,040	159	571	-301
Europe	1,581	2,017	2,622	1,966	674	279	4,489
China	300	124	117	531	358	354	226
Korea	239	317	250	186	80	342	618
ASEAN	884	1,354	1,107	3,397	1,381	5,903	8,339
Malaysia	141	278	232	1,018	313	340	-30
Singapore	741	1,077	836	2,297	1,016	5,479	8,229
Other	25	20	436	597	174	950	786
Total	**8,338**	**4,914**	**6,928**	**9,318**	**4,877**	**13,304**	**19,242**

Source: Bank Indonesia

Table 3. FDI by Country of Origin in total percentage

	2005	2006	2007	2008	2009	2010	2011
Japan	18.5	21.5	16.3	12.3	18.4	28.0	27.0
U.S.	41.3	-11.2	15.8	11.2	3.3	4.3	-1.6
Europe	19.0	41.0	37.8	21.1	13.8	2.1	23.3
China	3.6	2.5	1.7	5.7	7.3	2.7	1.2
Korea	2.9	6.5	3.6	2.0	1.6	2.6	3.2
ASEAN	10.6	27.5	16.0	36.5	28.3	44.4	43.3
Malaysia	1.7	5.6	3.3	10.9	6.4	2.6	-0.2
Singapore	8.9	21.9	12.1	24.7	20.8	41.2	42.8
Other	0.3	0.4	6.3	6.4	3.6	7.1	4.1
Total	100.0	100.0	100.0	100.0	100.0	100.0	100.0

Source: Bank Indonesia.

Table 4. FDI by Type of Investment in USD million

	2005	2006	2007	2008	2009	2010	2011
Equity Capital	5,129	2,451	5,252	8,033	4,358	7,895	10,429
Reinvested Earnings	2,683	2,164	2,294	1,070	621	4,105	3,922
Other Capital	525	298	-619	215	-104	1,303	4,891
Total	**8,338**	**4,914**	**6,928**	**9,318**	**4,877**	**13,303**	**19,242**

Source: Bank Indonesia.

Table 5. FDI by Industry and Country of Origin in USD million

	2005	2006	2007	2008	2009	2010	2011
Agriculture, Hunting, and Forestry	**2**	**225**	**286**	**197**	**-52**	**286**	**284**
Japan	0	3	0	-4	1	12	20
U.S.	9	-2	5	0	0	0	0
European Union	-36	183	185	10	-157	34	15
China	4	-4	6	7	21	-24	0
ASEAN	2	-2	-8	0	-5	0	237
Other	0	-2	15	7	16	-12	12
Mining & Quarrying	**1,226**	**322**	**1,904**	**3,610**	**1,302**	**1,896**	**3,882**
Japan	182	83	341	546	-78	84	-101
U.S.	165	34	1,262	1,056	177	430	-435
European Union	218	37	405	617	392	404	3,593
China	239	123	170	534	357	354	150
ASEAN	32	-142	113	614	144	186	418
Other	295	277	-50	228	295	272	266

Table 5. (Continued)

	2005	2006	2007	2008	2009	2010	2011
Electricity, Gas, and Water Supply	**162**	**-1**	**-61**	**-56**	**53**	**204**	**364**
Japan	-14	-7	16	0	0	63	253
European Union	176	-13	-76	4	9	135	60
ASEAN	0	19	-1	-66	31	4	14
Other	0	0	0	8	1	8	8
Manufacturing	**5,264**	**1,691**	**2,412**	**2,322**	**1,573**	**4,971**	**8,157**
Japan	182	83	341	546	-78	84	4,359
U.S.	165	34	1,262	1,056	177	430	112
European Union	647	819	1,128	991	185	-1,016	-623
China	46	0	8	-4	1	1	33
ASEAN	627	423	397	989	531	1,722	3,013
Other	-90	-49	45	-230	-49	814	500
Wholesale & Retail	**60**	**375**	**215**	**1,159**	**73**	**2,463**	**2,882**
Japan	25	30	-23	86	74	133	385
U.S.	9	-13	-20	-1	-8	0	0
Construction	**130**	**85**	**195**	**24**	**7**	**-49**	**86**
Japan	2	21	6	0	-1	10	94
U.S.	0	-14	-6	0	0	0	88
European Union	125	31	27	0	-1	0	91
China	0	0	0	0	0	2	95
ASEAN	2	35	24	14	-5	-23	97
Other	0	-14	-6	0	0	0	102
Others	**301**	**599**	**37**	**212**	**-11**	**654**	**-353**
Japan	354	166	-123	-13	13	61	85
U.S.	2	-3	-1	8	3	-7	-8
European Union	-32	86	183	6	-86	10	-15
China	0	-1	-62	0	0	0	0
ASEAN	-72	339	27	-4	26	122	121
Other	26	7	18	159	26	419	-619
TOTAL	**8,338**	**4,914**	**6,928**	**9,318**	**4,877**	**13,304**	**19,242**

Source: Bank Indonesia.

Table 6. FDI Realization by Region in Indonesia in USD Million

	2005	2006	2007	2008	2009	2010	2011
Java	**7,251**	**4,413**	**8,498**	**13,567**	**9,370**	**11,499**	**12,325**
Jakarta	3,272	1,468	4,669	9,928	5,511	6,429	4,824
West Java	2,567	1,619	1,328	2,552	1,934	1,692	3,839
East Java	702	384	1,691	457	422	1,769	1,312
Banten	668	512	708	478	1,412	1,544	2,172
Kalimantan	**182**	**537**	**309**	**115**	**284**	**2,011**	**1,919**
East Kalimantan	39	405	160	13	80	1,092	602

	2005	2006	2007	2008	2009	2010	2011
Sumatera	**1,225**	**884**	**1,386**	**1,009**	**776**	**747**	**2,077**
Riau	796	585	724	461	252	87	212.3
Sulawesi	**145**	**14**	**80**	**65**	**142**	**859**	**715**
Nusa Tenggara	**103**	**110**	**57**	**96**	**234**	**503**	**953**
Bali	97	103	51	81	227	278	482
Maluku	**9**	**20**	**0**	**0**	**6**	**249**	**142**
Papua	**0**	**1**	**2**	**19**	**2**	**347**	**1,345**
Total	**8,915**	**5,977**	**10,350**	**14,870**	**10,815**	**16,215**	**19,475**
% of GDP	**3.1**	**1.6**	**2.4**	**2.9**	**2.0**	**2.3**	**2.3**

Source: Investment Coordinating Board (BKPM).

In: Mexico, Indonesia, South Korea, and Turkey ISBN: 978-1-62618-863-1
Editor: Andres Salazar

Chapter 3

2013 Investment Climate Statement: Republic of Korea (Official Name of South Korea)*

Bureau of Economic and Business Affairs

The Republic of Korea (ROK) has made tremendous economic gains, transforming itself from a recipient of foreign assistance to a high technology manufacturing powerhouse and middle-income donor country in a generation. South Korea experienced slower-than-expected real GDP growth of 2 percent growth in 2012, largely due to the effect of the global economic downturn on its export-oriented economy. Growth is expected to remain moderate in coming years, due to the ROK's relatively developed economy, an aging population, and inflexible labor markets. Nonetheless, the ROK has so far weathered the global economic uncertainty and continues to remain a generally favorable destination for foreign investment. Following the 1997-98 Asian financial crisis, South Korea made significant progress in reforming its financial institutions and capital markets. In addition, the Korean government took steps to strengthen its competitiveness, enacting measures to boost foreign investment incentives and allow non-Koreans to own land and real property. With these changes, most Koreans recognize foreign investment as positive for the nation's development, despite continuing protectionist sentiment among certain elements of society. The highest levels of the Korean

* This is an edited, reformatted and augmented version of Bureau of Economic and Business Affairs, dated February 2013.

government remain committed to ensuring a level playing field for foreign investors. However, in the months prior to the December 2012 presidential elections, both domestic and foreign businesses experienced increased scrutiny from regulatory agencies, including pressure to control prices. President-elect Park Geun-hye has pledged to promote "economic democratization," including strengthening regulation of family-run conglomerates (chaebol), increasing support for small and medium enterprises, and increasing social welfare spending. It is unclear at this point how such policies may affect the investment climate.

Capital inflows quickly recovered following the 2008-09 global financial crisis and rose from USD 11.5 billion in 2009 to USD 13.1 billion in 2010. Inbound foreign direct investment (FDI) rose to USD 16.3 billion in 2012, up 19 percent from 2011, and was a record high for capital inflow. Foreign investment in all industries except the real estate sector increased last year, including a notable 31.7 percent increase in FDI in the service sector. The real estate sector has been stagnant throughout 2012. Global liquidity was the main driver of the investment increase. The ROK's recent sovereign debt rating hikes, reflecting its strong fiscal fundamentals, ability to withstand domestic risks and external shocks, and continuation of status quo in North-South Korea geopolitics, also served to burnish the ROK's reputation as a favorable destination for foreign investment. Household debt, while not a threat to the overall economy, has emerged as a growing social concern.

The United States retains the largest single-country share of FDI in Korea, totaling USD 49.8 billion or 24.5 percent of Korea's total stock of FDI since the 1960's. Japan has invested USD 32.8 billion (16.1 percent of the total), followed by the Netherlands with USD 21.7 billion (10.7 percent). EU countries have invested USD 67.4 billion or 33.1 percent of the total. Japan contributed the largest share of FDI in 2012, at USD 4.54 billion, a 98 percent increase from the previous year, due to extra liquidity produced by quantitative easing policies and a desire to diversify supply chains post-Fukushima. The United States recorded USD 3.67 billion of FDI in 2012, while EU contributed USD 2.69 billion; both contributions were less than the half of their investment in 2011. The IT, auto parts, logistics, and other service sectors are expected to absorb the majority of FDI in Korea in the near future, largely through mergers and acquisitions (M&A), in line with global trends.

In recent years, foreign portfolio investment has continued to increase. At the end of 2012, foreign shareholders owned 34.7 percent of Korean Stock Exchange stocks and 8.2 percent of the tech-heavy KOSDAQ Index shares.

Improvement in the consistency of the ROK Government's (ROKG) interpretation, transparency, and timeliness in the application of FDI regulations would enhance the investor climate in Korea. Unclear and opaque regulatory decision-making remained a significant concern, which can discourage FDI by creating uncertainty for investors and fostering an impression that the ROK remains hostile to foreign investment. Investors were also concerned about small but significant interest groups that pressure the government to protect the South Korean market from what is perceived as foreign domination. Regarding labor, South Korea boasts a hard-working, educated and highly productive workforce and high levels of institutional labor protections, but foreign investors cited volatility in labor-management relations as an issue that can hamper FDI.

The Korea-US (KORUS) Free Trade Agreement (FTA), which entered into force on 15 March 2012, is a major step forward in enhancing the legal framework for U.S. investors in South Korea. All forms of investment are protected under the FTA, including enterprises, debt, concessions and similar contracts, and intellectual property rights. With very few exceptions, U.S. investors will be treated the same as South Korean investors (or investors of any other country) in the establishment, acquisition, and operation of investments in Korea. In addition, these protections are backed by a transparent international arbitration mechanism, under which investors may, at their own initiative, bring claims against the government for an alleged breach of the investment. Submissions to investor-state arbitration tribunals as well as their hearings will be made public.

Openness to Foreign Investment

The Korean government's attitude toward foreign direct investment is positive, and senior policy makers clearly realize the value of FDI. Following the 2008-09 global financial crisis, FDI has continued to increase steadily, with USD 13.7 billion in 2011 and USD 16.3 billion in 2012.

Despite these improvements, FDI in South Korea is still at times subject to insufficient regulatory transparency, including inconsistent and sudden changes in interpretation of regulations, as well as underdeveloped corporate governance, high labor costs, an inflexible labor system, and lingering economic domination by chaebol.

All companies operating in South Korea, including foreign ones, were subject to pressure from ROKG agencies to maintain stable prices of certain items, including food, in the months leading up to the 2012 presidential election. Companies that benefited from KORUS or the Korea-EU FTA were also asked by ROKG agencies to demonstrate how they decreased prices of goods to reflect tariff cuts.

The Foreign Investment Promotion Act (FIPA) is the basic law pertaining to foreign investment in Korea. FIPA and related regulations categorize business activities as either open, conditionally or partly restricted, or closed to foreign investment. Restrictions remain for 27 industrial sectors, three of which are entirely closed to foreign investment. The South Korean government reviews restricted sectors from time to time for possible further openings. According to the Ministry of Knowledge Economy (MKE), the number of industrial sectors open to foreign investors is well above the OECD average.

FIPA features include:

- Simplified procedures, including those for FDI notification and registration;
- Expanded tax incentives for high-technology FDI;
- Reduced rental fees and lengthened lease durations for government land (including local government land);
- Increased central government support for local FDI incentives;
- Establishment of "Invest Korea," a one-stop investment promotion center within the Korea Trade Promotion Corporation to assist foreign investors;
- Establishment of an Ombudsman office to assist foreign investors.

MKE published a 2011 Consolidated Public Notice, updating new code numbers and titles for business sectors in accordance to the ninth revision of the Korea Standard Industry Code (KSIC). According to the 2009 Notice, the number of KSIC industrial classifications of business sectors increased from 1,121 to 1,145 and by the reclassification, business sectors where foreign investment is restricted increased from 28 to 29. There was no further modification in the recent MKE notice on May 2, 2012.

The following is a current list of Restricted Sectors for Foreign Investment. Figures in parentheses denote the Korean Industrial Classification Code:

Completely Closed

- Nuclear power generation (35111)
- Radio broadcasting (60100)
- Television broadcasting (60210)

Restricted Sectors (partly open not more than 25 percent)

- News agency activities (63910)

Restricted Sectors (partly open not more than 30 percent)

- Hydro electronic power generation (35112)
- Thermal power generation (35113)
- Other power generation (35119)

Restricted Sectors (partly open less than 30 percent)

- Publishing of newspapers (58121)

Restricted Sectors (partly open less than 49 percent)

- Satellite and other broadcasting (60229)
- Program distribution (60221)
- Cable networks (60222)
- Wired telephone and other telecommunications (61210)
- Mobile telephone and other telecommunications (61220)
- Satellite telephone and other telecommunications (61230)
- Other telecommunications (61299)

Restricted Sectors (partly open not more than 50 percent)

- Farming of beef cattle (01212)
- Inshore and coastal fishing (03112)
- Transmission/distribution of electricity (35120)
- Wholesale of meat (46312)
- Coastal water passenger transport (50121)
- Coastal water freight transport (50122)
- Publishing of magazines and periodicals (58122)

Open but Regulated under the Relevant Laws

- Growing of cereal crops and other food crops except rice and barley (01110)
- Domestic commercial banking except special banking area (64121)
- Radioactive waste collection, transportation, and disposal except radioactive waste management (38240)
- Other inorganic chemistry production except fuel for nuclear power generation (20129)
- Other nonferrous metals refining, smelting, and alloying (24219)

In categories open to investment, foreign exchange banks must be notified in advance of applications for foreign investment. All South Korean banks are permitted to deal in foreign exchange, including branches of foreign banks. In effect, these notifications are pro-forma, and approval can be processed within three hours. Applications may be denied only on specific grounds, including national security, public order and morals, international security obligations, and health and environmental concerns. Exceptions to the advance notification approval system exist for project categories subject to joint-venture requirements and certain projects in the distribution sector.

Relevant ministries must still approve investments in conditionally or partly restricted sectors. Most applications are processed within five days; cases that require consultation with more than one ministry can take 25 days or longer. Korea's procurement complies with the WTO Government Procurement Agreement, but some implementation problems remain.

Restrictions on foreign ownership of public corporations remain, although ownership limit levels have been raised. Currently, foreign ownership is limited for government-controlled utilities. Foreign ownership in South Korean telecommunications companies and cable networks is limited to 49 percent. The ROKG government intends to privatize many of the remaining state-owned corporations, but this process was slowed by the global financial crisis.

The Ministry of Strategy and Finance (MOSF) administers tax and other incentives to stimulate advanced technology transfer and investment in high-technology services. There are three types of special areas for foreign investment, including Free Economic Zones, Free Investment Zones, and Tariff Free Zones, where favorable tax incentives and other support for investors are available (see Section VI.)

South Korea's rankings in various international indices on corruption and business environment are as follows:

Measure	Year	Index/Ranking
Transparency International Corruption Index	2012	56*/45
	2011	5.4/43

* Note: The Transparency International Corruption Perceptions Index ranks countries and territories based on how corrupt their public sector is perceived to be; the scale for scores changed to 1-100 in 2012, whereas it was 1-10 in 2011 and prior years. A score of 0 means that a country is perceived as highly corrupt and 100 (or 10, in previous years) means it is perceived as very clean. The 2012 rank indicates the country's position relative to the 176 countries and territories in the index; the 2011 index included 182 countries and territories. Additional information is available at http://www.transparency.

Heritage Foundation Economic Freedom Index	2013	70.3/34
	2012	69.9/31

Note: The Heritage Foundation Economic Index ranks countries on a scale of 0 - 100, where 0 means that a country is perceived as economically repressed and 100 means it is perceived as economically free. In 2013, Heritage Foundation assessed ROK as "mostly free," with a ranking of 70.3 out of 100, and the ROK was considered the 34th freest country out of 177 countries ranked. Additional information is available at http://www.heritage.org/index/ranking.

World Bank Doing Business Index	2013	NA/9
	2012	NA/8

Note: The World Bank Doing Business Index is a ranking of 185 economies (in 2013). A high ranking means the regulatory environment is more conducive to the starting and operation of a local firm. Additional information is available at http://www.doingbusiness.org/rankings.

Basic Investment Rights

Conversion and Transfer Policies: According to the Foreign Exchange Transaction Act (FETA), only transactions that could harm international peace or public order, such as money laundering and gambling, are controlled. Three specific types of transactions are restricted:

1) Non-residents are not permitted to buy won-denominated hedge funds, including forward currency contracts;

2) The Financial Services Commission will not permit foreign currency borrowing by "non-viable" domestic firms; and
3) The Korean government will monitor and ensure that Korean firms that have extended credit to foreign borrowers collect their debts. The Korean government has retained the authority to re-impose restrictions in the case of severe economic or financial emergency.

Capital account liberalization under the Foreign Exchange Transaction Act (FETA) has also been extensive. All capital-account transactions are permitted unless specifically prohibited. In addition, 72 of the 91 transactions specified by the OECD code of liberalization of capital movements now are permitted. Non-residents may open deposit accounts in domestic currency (South Korean won) with maturities of more than one year and may engage in offshore transactions and issue won-denominated securities abroad.

The right to remit profits is granted at the time of original investment approval. Banks control the now *pro forma* approval process for FETA-defined open sectors. For conditionally or partially restricted investments (as defined by the FETA), the relevant ministry must provide approval for both investment and remittance.

When foreign investment royalties or other payments are proposed as part of a technology licensing agreement, the agreement and the projected stream of royalties must be approved either by a bank or MOSF. Approval is virtually automatic. An investor wishing to enact a remittance must present an audited financial statement to a bank to substantiate the payment. To withdraw capital, a stock valuation report issued by a recognized securities company or the Korean appraisal board also must be presented. Foreign companies seeking to remit funds from investments in restricted sectors must first seek ministerial and bank approval, after demonstrating the legal source of the funds and proving that relevant taxes have been paid.

Expropriation and Compensation

The ROK follows generally accepted principles of international law with respect to expropriation. Korean law protects foreign-invested enterprise property from expropriation or requisition. If private property is expropriated, it can only be taken for a public purpose and only in a non-discriminatory manner. Property owners are entitled to prompt compensation at fair market value. U.S. Embassy Seoul is not aware of any cases of uncompensated expropriation of property owned by American citizens.

Dispute Resolution

There exists a body of South Korean law governing commercial activities and bankruptcies that constitutes the means to enforce property and contractual rights, with monetary judgments usually levied in the domestic currency. The number of serious investment disputes involving foreigners has been limited in South Korea. Foreign court judgments are not enforceable in the ROK.

Over the past several years, we have seen a few high-profile cases involving U.S. firms that have had difficulty exiting the Korean market; these cases have increased concerns of other potential U.S. investors. Although commercial disputes can be adjudicated in a civil court, foreign businesses often feel that this is not a practical means to resolve disputes. Proceedings are conducted in Korean, often without adequate translation. South Korean law prohibits foreign lawyers who have not passed the Korean Bar Examination from representing clients in Korean courts. Civil procedures common in the United States, such as pretrial discovery, do not exist in South Korea. During litigation of a dispute, foreigners may be barred from leaving the country until a decision is reached. Legal proceedings are expensive and time-consuming and lawsuits often are contemplated only as a last resort, signaling the end of a business relationship.

Commercial disputes may also be taken to the Korean Commercial Arbitration Board (KCAB). The Korean Arbitration Act and its implementing rules outline the following steps in the arbitration process: 1) parties may request the KCAB to act as informal intermediary to a settlement; 2) if unsuccessful, either or both parties may request formal arbitration, in which case the KCAB appoints a mediator to conduct conciliatory talks for 30 days; and 3) if unsuccessful, an arbitration panel consisting of one or three arbitrators is assigned to decide the case. If one party is not resident in Korea, either may request an arbitrator from a neutral country.

When drafting contracts, it may be useful to provide for arbitration by a neutral body such as the International Commercial Arbitration Association (ICAA). U.S. companies should seek local expert legal counsel when drawing up any type of contract with a South Korean entity.

The ROK is a member of the International Center for the Settlement of Investment Disputes (ICSID). It has also acceded to the United Nations

Convention on the Recognition and Enforcement of Foreign Arbitral Awards (New York Convention). Korea is a member of the International Commercial Arbitration Association and the World Bank's Multilateral Investment Guarantee Agency (MIGA). South Korean courts may ultimately be called upon to enforce an arbitrated settlement.

PERFORMANCE REQUIREMENTS AND INCENTIVES

South Korea does not maintain any measures notified to the World Trade Organization (WTO) as being inconsistent with (or that are alleged to be inconsistent with) the WTO Agreement on Trade-Related Investment Measures (TRIMs Agreement). The ROK ceased imposing performance requirements on new foreign investment in 1989 and eliminated all pre-existing performance requirements in 1992. The ROKG has no requirement that investors purchase from local sources or export a certain percentage of output. There is no ROKG requirement that Korean nationals must own shares in foreign investments or that technology be transferred on certain terms. The Korean government does not impose "offset" requirements on investors to invest in specific manufacturing, R&D, or service facilities. There are also no government-imposed conditions on permission to invest.

The Korean government allows the following general incentives for foreign investors:

- Cash grants for the creation and expansion of workplaces for high-tech business plants and R&D (research and development) centers;
- Reduced rent for land and site preparation for foreign investors;
- Grants for establishment of convenience facilities for foreigners;
- Reduced rent for state or public property; and
- Preferential financial support for investing in major infrastructure projects.

RIGHT TO PRIVATE OWNERSHIP AND ESTABLISHMENT

Korea fully recognizes rights of private ownership and has a well-developed body of laws governing the establishment of corporate and other business enterprises. Private entities may freely acquire and dispose of assets;

however, the Fair Trade Act may limit cross-ownership of shares in two or more firms if the effect is to restrict competition in a particular industry.

The Alien Land Acquisition Act (amended in 1998) grants non-resident foreigners and foreign corporations the same rights as Koreans in purchasing and using land. The Real Estate Investment Trust (REIT) Act supports sound indirect investments in real estate and restructuring of corporations. The REIT Act allows investors to invest funds through an asset management company, and in real property such as office buildings, business parks, shopping malls, hotels, and serviced apartments.

Almost no restrictions remain on foreign ownership of stock in Korean firms. Korean law permits foreign direct investment through mergers and acquisitions with existing domestic firms, including hostile takeovers. Nonetheless, no hostile takeovers have occurred in Korea in part because of the lack of relevant implementation regulations for the Foreign Investment Promotion Act. In addition, the political environment for hostile takeovers remains unfriendly.

Protection of Property Rights (Including Intellectual Property)

The ROK's progress on intellectual property rights (IPR) led to its removal from the Special 301 Watch List in 2009. Since then, the ROK has remained off the Watch List and demonstrated continued commitment to strong IPR enforcement. The importance that the ROK government places on IPR protection has increased dramatically in recent years as the digitization of Korea's economy has significantly enhanced the ability to produce and spread unauthorized reproductions of copyrighted material. With Korea's products and trademarks enjoying global success, Korean creators of intellectual property stand to benefit from improvements in the domestic intellectual property protection regime. The KORUS FTA contains state-of-the-art protections for all types of intellectual property, requirements to join key multilateral IPR agreements, and strong enforcement provisions. However, concerns remain over new forms of online piracy, corporate end-user software piracy, unauthorized use of software in the public sector, book piracy in universities, and counterfeiting of consumer products.

The ROK amended its copyright law in 2011 to conform to commitments under the Korea-EU and KORUS FTAs. Subordinate regulations including presidential and ministerial decrees were also amended to implement the Act in 2011. The amendment of the Copyright Act extended from 20 years to 70 years of copyright protection for works produced between July 1, 1988 and June 30, 1994.

In 2011, the Korea Communications Commission (KCC) passed the Telecommunications Business Act and its presidential decree requiring registration of webhard [online storage sites] and P2P with the KCC to address technical challenges related to online copyright enforcement.

Under the "three strikes" law, the Ministry of Culture, Sports and Tourism (MCST) can order online service providers (OSPs) to issue warning letters to users illegally downloading materials and require such users to delete illegal files. In the event that an OSP failed to comply with corrective recommendation issued by KCC and three warning letters have been issued, the user's account will be suspended temporarily. In 2012, MCST did not issue any warning letters and there was no temporary suspension of user accounts as OSPs all complied with the corrective recommendations issued by KCC, according to MCST. KCC's issuance of corrective recommendations has increased significantly over the years: 35,345 in 2009, 85,085 in 2010, 107,724 in 2011, and 250,039 in 2012.

Under the Information and Telecommunication Network Act, MCST took unprecedented steps to block access to illegal file-sharing sites. MCST requested KCC to block service to a total of 30 OSPs in 2012, down from 237 OSPs in 2011. Most of the sites were hosted on overseas servers – 16 music and film sites, 2 game servers, and 12 smart phone applications. Although many of the sites can migrate to other servers, the action marked an important shift in Korea's efforts to combat piracy. MCST made use of the Telecommunications Act to block access to such illegal file-sharing sites, whereas in the past, the Telecommunications Act has solely been used to restrict traffic to pornographic or North Korea-related online material.

Through the Copyright Protection Center, MCST deleted 176.4 million illegal online files in 2012, up from 86.3 million files in 2011. MCST collected and destroyed 639,290 offline items in 2012, up from 269,409 items in 2011.

MCST held its fifth annual 100-day campaign against off-line pirated copyrighted material, known as the "100-Day Clean Seoul Project," from April to August, 2012. During the 2012 campaign, MCST and Korean law enforcement raided street vendors and stores selling pirated DVDs, CDs, software, and books. According to MCST's statistics, authorities seized 217,881 pirated items, up from 79,909 items in 2011. In addition, MCST investigated Korean university campuses and confiscated 16,547 illegally copied books, up from 13,212 books in 2011.

MCST Judicial Police conducted software enforcement at 596 companies in 2012 and found damages amounting to 15.7 billion won (14.8 million USD), with a piracy rate of 35.36 percent. In 2011, MCST raided 1,028 companies and found damages amounting to 15.5 billion won (14.6 million USD), with a piracy rate of 30 percent.

Lastly, MCST recommended 1,803 IPR related cases for legal action in 2012, up from 1,115 cases in 2011. Out of the 1,803 cases, prosecutors secured indictments for 541 cases, up from 313 cases in 2011. Among the 541 case, 436 were for online piracy, 34 for off-line piracy and 71 for software infringement.

LABOR

According to the Ministry of Employment and Labor (MOEL), there were approximately 25 million economically active persons in ROK with an employment rate (OECD standard) of approximately 60 percent. The overall unemployment rate of 2.8 percent in 2012 was much lower than the unemployment rate of youth aged 15-29, which at 7.5 percent is becoming a domestic concern. Since 2004, South Korea has implemented a "guest worker" program known as the Employment Permit System (EPS) to help protect the rights of foreign workers. EPS allows employers to legally employ a certain number of foreign workers from 15 countries, including the Philippines, Indonesia, and Vietnam, with which the ROK maintains bilateral labor agreements. For 2013, South Korea increased its quota to 62,000 migrant workers. At the end of October 2012, approximately 490,000 foreigners were said to be working under EPS in manufacturing, construction, agriculture, livestock, service, and fishery industries.

Korean law provides workers with the right to associate freely and allows public servants to organize unions. The labor law was amended in 2011 to authorize union pluralism. The 2010 revision of Trade Union and Labor Relations Adjustment Act (TULRA), which became law in 2011, restricted the number of full-time labor union officials and banned employers from paying wages to such officials for union work. The TULRA revision also allowed the formation of multiple unions at the same workplace, but required only one bargaining channel. The ratio of organized labor to the entire population of wage earners at the end of 2011 was 10.1 percent; this ratio has remained relatively stable over the last ten years or so. Korea's trade union participation is lower than the latest-available OECD average of 17.5 percent in 2011; more information is available at http://stats.oecd.org/Index.aspx?DataSet Code= UN_DEN.

The country has three national labor federations. The Korean Confederation of Trade Unions (KCTU) has 2,362 labor unions and about 770,000 members and the Federation of Korean Trade Unions (FKTU) has 415 labor unions and 560,000 members. KCTU and FKTU are affiliated with the International Trade Union Confederation (ITUC). Most of FKTU's constituent unions maintained affiliations with international union federations. The Korean Labor Union Confederation (KLUC) is the smallest and newest federation, with only 87 unions and about 20,000 members, and attracts those seeking a trade union that is neither militant nor political. There are 2,256 unions with 370,000 workers who do not belong to a nationwide federation but rather focus just on their corporate issues.

The law provides for the right to collective bargaining and collective action, and workers exercise these rights in practice. The law also empowers workers to file complaints of unfair labor practices against employers who interfere with union organizing or who discriminate against union members. The National Labor Relations Commission can require employers found guilty of unfair practices to reinstate workers fired for engaging in union activities.

Labor organizations are permitted in export processing zones (EPZs), but foreign companies operating in EPZs are exempt from some labor regulations. Exemptions include provisions that mandate paid leave, requiring companies with more than 50 persons to recruit persons with disabilities for at least 2 percent of their workforce, encouraging companies to reserve 3 percent of their workforce for workers over 55 years of age, and restricting large companies from participating in certain business categories.

The Labor Standards Act prohibits the employment of persons under age 15 without an employment authorization certificate from MOEL. Because education is compulsory through middle school (approximately age 15), few employment authorization certificates were issued for full-time employment. To obtain employment, children under age 18 must obtain written approval from either parents or guardians. Employers must limit minors' overtime hours and are prohibited from employing minors at night without special permission from MOEL.

The minimum wage is reviewed annually. Labor and business set the minimum wage for 2013 at 4,860 won (approximately $4.54) per hour, a 6.1 percent increase from last year that is relatively in line with the 3.4 percent increase in the minimum cost of living. The Labor Standards Act also provides for a 50 percent higher wage for overtime.

The government sets health and safety standards, and the Korea Occupational Safety and Health Agency (KOSHA) is responsible for monitoring industry adherence to these standards. KOSHA conducts inspections both proactively according to regulations and reactively in response to complaints. It also provides technical assistance to resolve any deficiencies discovered during inspections. KOSHA reports on its website descriptions of and statistics on work-related injuries and fatalities biannually. From January through June 2012, there were 44,726 work-related accidents and 675 fatalities, a 0.7 percent increase and 1.2 percent increase respectively from the same period in 2011. KOSHA provides training and subsidies to improve work safety and reduce work-related accidents. Its services are extended to the migrant workers as its training modules and materials are available in 10 languages and disseminated to various worksites.

Contract and other "non-regular" workers accounted for a substantial portion of the workforce. MOEL reported that there were approximately 6.66 million non-regular workers, comprising approximately 26.7 percent of the total workforce as of November 2012. MOEL also reported that in 2011 non-regular workers performed work similar to regular workers but received approximately 87.4 percent of the wages of regular workers.

The Act for Part-Time and Temporary Workers' Protection prohibits the discrimination of non-regular workers and requires that non-regular workers employed longer than two years be converted to permanent status. The two-year rule went into effect on July 1, 2009. Both the labor and business sectors have complained that the two-year conversion law forced many businesses to limit the contract terms of the non-regular workers to two-years and incur the sunk cost for entry of new labor every two years.

Corporate Governance and Investment Decision-Making

Investors and financial markets remain wary of corporate governance in Korea despite significant improvements since the 1997-98 Asian financial crisis. Concerns about corporate governance often reduce the price to earnings ratios to levels lower than comparable companies elsewhere. Korean policy makers acknowledge that foreign investors often exact a "Korea Discount" when dealing with Korean companies or in making investment decisions. Large gaps continue to exist between the ownership and control of a significant number of firms in Korea, with many chaebol still controlled by their founding families, despite the family's relatively small ownership stakes. Increasing participation by foreign investors and stockholders, modernizing business-government relations, and infusing professionalism in the corporate culture would greatly help improve corporate governance.

Although the Anti-Monopoly and Fair Trade Act has been amended repeatedly – most recently in March 2012 – the practical impact of Korea's laws and policies regulating monopolistic practices and unfair competition, however, has been limited by the long-standing economic strength of the chaebol. Management control at the chaebol continues to involve complicated webs of cross-shareholdings among chaebol affiliates, and many chaebol still conduct business based on family and personal connections. Chaebol-government relations can also sometimes influence the business-government dialogue, to the detriment of foreign and small and medium-sized enterprises (SMEs). Thus, chaebol influence in the South Korean economy may sometimes cause practical business problems for foreign investors. SME suppliers, for example, may be reluctant to deal with foreign firms for fear of jeopardizing a prized chaebol relationship. Obtaining access to credit may be complicated by the privileged relationships competing chaebol enjoy with local banks, although this is mitigated by the fact that regulations limit a bank's exposure to any single chaebol group's companies to 25 percent of capital, and stipulate that at least 25 percent of all banks' lending must go to SMEs.

Foreign ownership is also playing a significant role in promoting corporate governance reform in Korea. Korean firms with significant foreign investment, for example, are generally understood to be more reluctant to participate in government-sponsored bailouts of troubled firms, impacting the evolution of Korean financial markets. As foreign investors now own about 60 percent of the shares in some of Korea's top companies and nearly 33 percent of stock listed on Korea's main stock exchange, the rights of minority and non-Korean stockholders are becoming more clearly expressed.

Under Korea's 2005 Securities Class Action Act, minority shareholders are able to file class action suits for manipulation of share prices, false disclosure of information, and accounting malpractice. However, in large part due to rather stringent and complex procedural requirements, only one class-action suit has been filed since the law came into effect.

The Korean government is currently implementing an accounting reform plan, taken largely from the U.S. Sarbanes-Oxley Act, aimed at making Korean accounting standards consistent with rigorous international standards. The International Financial Reporting Standards (K-IFRS) were adopted and implemented during the first quarter of 2011. In parallel, a committee of Korean private sector experts has established a Code of Best Practices in response to a tasking by the finance ministry. The voluntary recommendations included in this Code are in line with OECD principles, and the Korea Exchange (KRX) has reinforced the importance of the Code by requiring that companies listed on the Korea Stock Exchange (KSE) provide information to investors about the extent to which they conform to the Code. Following are some of the key recommendations contained in the Code of Best Practices:

- Easing of ownership thresholds to allow small shareholders greater rights to inspect company books;
- Having outside or independent directors make up at least half (rather than a quarter) of the board members of listed companies;
- Establishing a nominating committee to choose board members, with at least half of the committee consisting of outside directors;
- Ensuring that outside directors are truly independent, with no interests in the company, the management, or the controlling shareholder;
- Having the board of directors meet at least once every three months; and
- Requiring that companies have audit committees consisting of at least three directors, of which two-thirds are outside directors.

Transparency of the Regulatory System

The Korean regulatory environment can pose challenges for all firms, both foreign and domestic. Laws and regulations are often framed in general terms and are subject to differing interpretations by government officials, who rotate frequently. Regulations are sometimes promulgated with only minimal consultation with industry and with only the minimally required comment period. The KORUS FTA includes many provisions designed to address such issues.

According to Korea's Administrative Procedures Act, proposed laws and regulations (Acts, Presidential Decrees or Ministerial Decrees) should be published and public comments solicited for at least 40 days prior to promulgation. Draft bills are often available on the web sites of relevant ministries without notice that they have been published. The rule-making process often remains non-transparent, particularly for foreigners. Proposed rules are sometimes published with insufficient time to permit public comment and industry adjustment. For example, regulatory changes originating from legislation proposed by members of Korea's National Assembly are not subject to public comment periods. When notifications of proposed rules are made public, they usually appear in the Official Gazette, but not consistently, and only in the Korean language; thus, much of the 40-day comment period can be exhausted translating complex documentation.

The Korean government may restrict investments that disrupt production of military products or equipment, or if the company the foreigner is investing in exports items that may be later used for military purposes differing from their originally intended use. Foreigners linked to a country or an organization that may pose a threat to national security will also be subject to limitations on their investments in Korean firms. Related government agencies must ask MKE to review the case within 30 days of a foreign investor filing an application for regulatory approval, and MKE must make a decision within the following 90 days.

The World Economic Forum (WEF) 2012-13 Global Competitive Index ranked Korea 19th overall in global competitiveness, among 144 nations surveyed, an improvement from its ranking of 24 in 2011-12. The 2012-13 report cited persistent concerns in the quality of its institutions, its labor market efficiency, and its financial market development, even though the ROK posted improvement in these three areas. For more information, visit http://reports.weforum.org/global-competitiveness-report-2012-2013.

Capital Markets and Portfolio Investment

Financial sector reforms are often cited as one reason for the ROK's rapid rebound from the 2008 global financial crisis. Financial sector reforms have aimed to increase transparency and investor confidence and generally purge the sector of moral hazard. Since 1998, the Korean government has recapitalized its banks and non-bank financial institutions, closed or merged weak financial institutions, resolved many non-performing assets, introduced internationally-accepted risk assessment methods and accounting standards for banks, forced depositors and investors to assume appropriate levels of risk, and taken steps to help end the policy-directed lending of the past. These reforms addressed weak supervision and poor lending practices in the Korean banking system that helped cause and exacerbate the 1997-98 Asian financial crisis.

In the course of stabilizing Korea's banking sector during the Asian financial crisis, the Korean government injected public funds, thereby acquiring *de facto* ownership of many of Korea's commercial banks, although it publicly committed to refrain from interfering in bank lending and management decisions, except with regard to prudential supervision. In late 2002, the Korean government began its ambitious plan to re-privatize the banks under its control, with the program initially scheduled to end by the first quarter of 2005. Much of this re-privatization has taken place, although the government continues to own the majority of shares in Woori Bank and minority shares in some other banks. Foreign banks are allowed to establish subsidiaries or direct branches. Further relaxation of regulations has widened foreign access to Korea's capital markets and permitted foreign financial firms to engage in non-hostile mergers and acquisitions of local financial institutions. The National Assembly in 2010 amended the Bank Act to: (1) require banks to have outside directors constitute the majority of directors; and (2) forbid majority shareholders and related individuals from being outside directors.

South Korea routinely permits the repatriation of funds, but reserves the right to limit capital outflows in exceptional circumstances, such as situations when uncontrolled outflows might harm the balance of payments, cause excessive fluctuations in interest or exchange rates, or threaten the stability of domestic financial markets. The Korean government did not impose such restrictions either during the Asian financial crisis or the global financial crisis, where sharp capital outflows played a major role. However, the government has installed a series of capital control measures under the name of "macro-prudential stability policy," which includes lowering foreign exchange forward-position limits for foreign bank branches in 2010, re-introducing a withholding tax on foreign investors' government bond purchases, and imposing a bank levy on non-deposit financing in foreign currency from August 2011. On December 3, 2012, the government lowered the forward-position limits again and changed bank levy provisions to promote long-term financing.

Foreign portfolio investors now enjoy good access to the ROK stock market. Aggregate foreign investment ceilings in the Korean Stock Exchange (KSE) were abolished in 1998, and foreign investors owned 34.7 percent of KSE stocks and 8.2 percent of the Korean Securities Dealers Automated Quotations (KOSDAQ) as of the end of 2012. The market turnover rate was 338 percent of market capitalization in 2012. Retail investors are extremely active in the Korean stock markets. More than 80 percent of KSE and

KOSDAQ retail trading is conducted online. Thus, a large majority of retail investors are day traders, implying a constant source of volatility for the markets. The Korean government permits stock purchases on margin, requiring that transactions be settled within three business days.

Portfolio investors have shown less appetite for the smaller, more volatile, technology-rich KOSDAQ. Since the collapse of the Daewoo Group in 1999, Korea's largest corporate bankruptcy, the country's bond market has been almost moribund, as sellers have far outnumbered buyers. The total assets of Korea's commercial banks as of the end of September 2012 were 1,413 trillion won, or about USD 1.25 trillion.

Short-term interest rates, around 3 percent, remain comparatively high. Inflation, meanwhile, remained at 2.2 percent throughout 2012. The spread between short-term money (91-day CD rate) and long-term money (the benchmark 3-year corporate bond rate) fell to 40-plus basis points in 2012 from 66 basis points in 2011 as the global liquidity overflow continued. Concerned about inflation, the Bank of Korea (BOK) froze the benchmark rate at 3.25 percent for thirteen consecutive months from the second half of 2011 through the first half of 2012, even though inflationary pressure remained weak throughout the period. As economic growth again slowed due to the recent global economic downturn, the BOK cut the rate twice in the second half of 2012 to 2.75 percent.

COMPETITION FROM STATE-OWNED ENTERPRISES

Many South Korean state-owned enterprises (SOEs) continue to exert significant control over certain segments of the economy. By the end of 2002, major SOEs including Korea Telecom (KT), Pohang Iron and Steel Corporation (POSCO), Korea Tobacco and Ginseng Corporation (KT&G), Korea Heavy Industries and Construction Corporation were fully privatized. No SOEs have been privatized since 2002. The Lee Myung-bak administration called off most plans to restructure SOEs for reasons both political (conflict with labor unions) and economic (concern about the impact the privatizations would have on the economy in the midst of the global financial crisis). Today, there are 37 remaining SOEs in Korea, active in the energy, real estate, and infrastructure (railroad, highway construction) sectors. The law has traditionally sought to give SOEs a leading role in these sectors, but over the past several years, the government has increasingly tried to attract more private participation as well, especially in the real estate and construction sectors.

The Public Institutions Management Act (PIMA) gives authority to the Ministry of Strategy and Finance to administer control of many SOEs, mainly focusing on administrative and human resource management. SOEs subject to PIMA are required to report to a line minister; the President or line ministers appoint senior government officials or politically-affiliated individuals as CEOs or directors. SOEs are explicitly obligated to consult with government officials on their budget, compensation, and key management decisions (i.e. pricing policy for energy and public utilities). For other issues, the government officials informally require the SOEs to consult with them before making decision or report to them afterward.

The South Korean government does not provide any official data on SOEs' market shares. The ROKG requires each entity to disclose financial statements, the number of employees, and average compensation figures.

The Korea Investment Corporation (KIC), a sovereign wealth fund, was established in July 2005 under the KIC Act. KIC is wholly government-owned with an independent steering committee that has the authority to undertake core business decisions. KIC is on the PIMA list. Korea has no asset management bureau. KIC is mandated to manage assets entrusted by the Government and the BOK. Based on the continued increase in entrusted assets and gains realized on investments, assets under management stood at USD 50 billion at the end of August 2012.

KIC has no role in the local economy as it has only engaged in overseas investments to date. It is required by law to publish an annual report and to submit its books to the steering committee for review. KIC is also required to follow all domestic accounting standards and rules.

Corporate Social Responsibility in Korea

Corporate social responsibility (CSR) awareness is growing in Korea but is still in a nascent stage. For those South Korean firms that publish CSR reports, environmental impact, particularly on land and water resources, is the primary focus. Korean CSR reflects the continued impact of traditional notions of corporate CSR as charity. The Korean government is increasingly encouraging companies, including foreign subsidiaries and branches, to engage in CSR activities, particularly with the Administration's emphasis on shared growth.

Country Risk Issues

Political Violence

The Democratic People's Republic of Korea (DPRK, or North Korea) and the ROK technically remain in a state of war. There is general peace and stability on the Korean peninsula because of an armistice agreement that has lasted for close to 60 years. From time to time incidents involving military and political provocations have contributed to increased tension between the countries. For example, the unprovoked sinking of a ROK naval vessel by the DPRK in March 2010 and the artillery shelling of an island off the northwest coast of the ROK in November 2010 resulted in increased tensions. Military incidents have remained limited to the area surrounding the five geographically isolated Northwest Islands.

The ROK does not have a history of political violence directed against foreign investors. Embassy Seoul is unaware of any politically motivated threats of damage to foreign-invested projects or foreign-related installations of any sort, nor of any incidents that might be interpreted as having targeted foreign investments. Labor violence unrelated to the issue of foreign ownership, however, has occurred in foreign-owned facilities in the past.

Corruption

The law provides criminal penalties for official corruption, and the government generally implements these laws effectively. By law, public servants above a certain rank must register their assets, including how they were accumulated, thereby making their holdings public. According to the Transparency International Global Corruption Barometer 2010, only two percent of South Koreans had paid a bribe to receive attention from at least one of nine different service providers (in customs, education, the judiciary, land related services, medical services, the police, registry & permit services, tax authorities, and utilities) in the past 12 months. Of the 21 economies surveyed in the Asia Pacific with an average of 11 percent of the population with experience paying bribes, ROK enjoyed the lowest percentage along with Australia.

The ROK signed the United Nations Convention against Corruption on December 10, 2003 and ratified it on March 27, 2008. The ROK is also a party to the OECD Convention on Combating Bribery of Foreign Public Officials in

International Business Transactions, and a member of the Asia Pacific Economic Cooperation Anti-Corruption and Transparency Experts Task Force (APEC ACT).

There are several government agencies responsible for combating government corruption including the Board of Audit and Inspection, which monitors government expenditures and the Public Service Ethics Committee, which monitors the civil servants' financial disclosures and their financial activities within their tenure and first few years into their retirement. The Anti-Corruption and Civil Rights Commission manages the public complaints and administrative appeals on corrupt government practices. The Financial Intelligence Unit has cooperated fully with U.S. and United Nations efforts to identify and shut down sources of terrorist financing. Transparency International has maintained a National Chapter in the ROK since 1999.

Bilateral Investment Agreements

The United States has a bilateral Treaty of Friendship, Commerce, and Navigation with South Korea, which contains general provisions pertaining to business relations and investment. During former Korean President Kim Dae-jung's visit to the U.S. in 1998, President Clinton and President Kim agreed to negotiate a Bilateral Investment Treaty (BIT) between the two nations. However, negotiations in 1998 and 1999 stalled after the two sides could not resolve differences on certain issues. The KORUS FTA contains strong, enforceable investment provisions that went into force in March 2012.

OPIC and Other Investment Insurance Programs

U.S. investments in Korea are eligible for insurance programs sponsored by the U.S. Overseas Private Investment Corporation (OPIC). OPIC has not, however, guaranteed any U.S. investments in Korea since 1998, when OPIC reinstated coverage it had suspended in 1991 due to concerns about worker rights. Coverage issued prior to 1991 is still in force. Korea has been a member of the World Bank's (IBRD) Multilateral Investment Guarantee Agency (MIGA) since 1987.

Free Economic Zones and Free Trade Zones

The Foreign Investment Promotion Act (FIPA) is meant to support potential investors and create a business environment conducive to increased foreign investment. FIPA offers foreign investors various incentives including tax breaks and cash grants for projects. Korea aims to attract more foreign investment by promoting its six Free Economic Zones (FEZ): Incheon (near Incheon Airport, to be completed in 2020); Busan/Jinhae (in South Gyeongsan Province, to be completed in 2020); Gwangyang Bay (in South Gyeongsan Province, to be completed in 2020); Yellow Sea (in South Chungcheong Province, to be completed 2025); Daegu/Gyeongbuk (in North Gyeongsan Province, to be completed in 2020); and Saemangeum/Gunsan (in North Jeolla Province, to be completed in 2030). The FEZs differ from other zones designated for foreign investment in their focus on creating a comprehensive living and working environment with biotechnology, aviation, logistics, manufacturing, service and other industrial clusters as well as international schools, recreational facilities, and international hospitals. In 2009, the National Assembly passed the Special Act on Free Economic Zones to increase tax benefits for investment, increase the FEZ infrastructure budget, and streamline the approval process for land development. On December 28, 2010, the government announced a plan to abolish inefficient, underperforming, and unfeasible portions of the nation's free economic zones as part of its efforts to reorganize the specially created districts. By the plan, the Ministry of Knowledge Economy removed the FEZ status from 90.51 square kilometers (22,366 acres), or 15.9 percent of the total land in the zones in February 2012. According to the ministry, the six FEZs have attracted just USD 2.73 billion in investments since 2003, yet the country has spent 85.4 trillion won (USD 74.3 billion) on their infrastructure and promotion. Songdo City in the Incheon FEZ in 2012 won the right to host the UN's Green Climate Fund and aims to become an innovative, state-of-the-art Northeast Asia business hub. The city will be the first LEED (Leadership in Energy and Environmental Design) certified district in Korea and the largest project outside North America to be included in the LEED Neighborhood Development Pilot Program. It will offer commercial office space, residences, retail shops, hotels, schools, hospitals, and cultural facilities. Additional information is available at http://www.songdo.com.

There are also six foreign-exclusive industrial complexes in Korea in different parts of the country, designed to provide inexpensive plant sites, with the national and local governments providing assistance for leasing or selling in such sites at discounted rates. In addition, there are four Free Trade Zones in Iksan, Gunsan, Daebul, and Masan where companies may pursue their business with government support, but without the usual legal requirements such as approval procedures for export and imports and customs duties. There are also seven Foreign Investment Zones designated by local governments to accommodate industrial sites for foreign investors. Special considerations for foreign investors vary among these options. A good source of information on Korea's various free trade zones is the government-run "Invest Korea," an inward investment promotion organization under the Korea Trade and Investment Promotion Agency (KOTRA). More information is available here:

Invest Korea, KOTRA Bldg.
13, Heolleungno, Seocho-gu, Seoul, Republic of Korea
Tel: (82) 1600 – 7119; Fax: (82-2) 3497 – 1611
http://www.investkorea.org

In addition, the Korean government also continues to put significant effort into programs to enhance the quality of life in Korea for foreign investors and their families. There are 51 foreign schools in Korea and one big college (SUNY Korea) in the Incheon FEZ that opened its doors in March 2012. More information on international education is available at http://www.isi.go.kr.

Foreign Direct Investment Statistics

(USD Millions)	Annual Flow			Cumulative Stock
	2010	2011	2012	
Total Inward FDI	13,071	13,673	16,258	203,516
United States	1,974	2,372	3,674	49,829
China	414	651	727	4,464
EU	3,196	5,032	2,689	67,384
Japan	2,083	2,289	4,541	32,805
Others	5,404	3,329	4,627	49,034
Total Outward FDI*	33,060	36,357	30,678	317,898
United States	5,050	14,129	4,766	62,079
China	3,928	4,351	5,453	55,675
EU	7,452	1,519	3,334	40,105
Japan	344	209	628	4,851
Others	16,286	16,149	16,497	155,188

Note: Outward FDI figures are as of September, 2012. Source: The Export-Import Bank of Korea and Ministry of Knowledge Economy Note: This data is based on the notification of cases.

In: Mexico, Indonesia, South Korea, and Turkey ISBN: 978-1-62618-863-1
Editor: Andres Salazar

Chapter 4

2013 Investment Climate Statement: Turkey*

Bureau of Economic and Business Affairs

Turkey is the 17th largest economy in the world, with a GDP of USD 774.2 billion. Over the last three years, Turkey has been one of the fastest growing economies, with an ambitious target to become one of the ten largest economies in the world by 2023, the centenary of the foundation of the Turkish republic. Achieving this goal will require Turkey to triple its economy to more than USD 2 trillion, develop an export sector of USD 500 billion, and make significant upgrades to its energy, information technology, finance, and physical infrastructures. While this will be a challenge, Turkey has more than doubled the size of its economy since 1990 and transformed it from roughly 20% industrial/ 80% lightly processed or raw materials to 75% industrial and manufactured. Regardless of whether Turkey is able to become a top 10 economy by 2023, we believe many positive economic reforms will come out of trying to meet such an ambitious goal, and the U.S. strongly supports Turkey's efforts in this regard.

The Turkish Government announced a new investment incentive program in April 2012, which went into effect retroactively on January 1, 2012, aimed at encouraging strategic investments and investment in less developed regions in order to eliminate regional disparities, reduce Turkey's dependence on imported intermediate goods, and increase technology transfer. In December

* This is an edited, reformatted and augmented version of Bureau of Economic and Business Affairs, dated February 2013.

2012, the World Bank and the U.S. Department of Commerce hosted an "Ease of Doing Business" seminar for the Turkish interagency to help the Turkish Government understand what reforms are needed to make Turkey more investor friendly and competitive in the international arena. The seminar highlighted that Turkey still needs to improve overall governmental transparency, continue regulatory reforms, increase predictability in regulatory development, better protect intellectual property, and translate rules and regulations into action. The World Bank's Ease of Doing Business Index (http://www.doingbusiness.org/reports/global-reports/doing-business-2013), as well as the Heritage Foundation-Wall Street Journal's Index of Economic Freedom (http://www.heritage.org/index/country/Turkey), offer useful summaries of key issues regarding doing business in Turkey.

Turkey's economic growth will slow significantly in 2013, projected at 2.6%, due mainly from weakening demand in Turkey's main export market – the EU. As a result, Turkey is actively seeking new and expanded export markets in the Middle East, Africa, and the United States. Turkish exports are projected to be around USD 153 billion at the end of 2012, a 13% year-on-year increase. The Turkish Government has set its export target for 2013 at USD 158 billion.

Turkey's Current Account Deficit (CAD), which was around 8.5% of GDP at the end of 2011, declined significantly in 2012 and is expected to be 6.5-7% of GDP when final 2012 figures are released. This decline is mainly attributable to the decreasing foreign trade deficit, increasing net services income and decreasing net income outflows. Inflation increased to over 10% during 2012 but by the end of 2012 is expected to be around 6.5%. The Turkish Central Bank is aiming for an inflation rate of 5% in 2013. Due to these positive trends, in November 2012, Fitch Ratings upgraded Turkey to investment grade for the first time in almost two decades, citing a moderating debt burden, healthy banking system, and sound economic management. This should help to increase institutional investment in Turkey.

In Turkey, the proportion of urban to rural population has changed significantly over the last decade. Turkey has broadened the base of its economy beyond the traditional industrial centers of Istanbul, Ankara, and Izmir to encompass a number of other Anatolian cities that exported more than USD 1 billion in 2012. This expansion is particularly notable in cities such as Adana, Denizli, Trabzon, Gaziantep, Hatay, Kayseri, Konya, Manisa, Sakarya, and Şırnak.

Relations with the United States

In 2009, President Obama called for the elevation of U.S.-Turkey economic and commercial ties to the same strategic level as our security and political ties. In October 2010, the United States and Turkey held the first meeting of the Framework for Strategic Economic and Commercial Cooperation (FSECC), a Cabinet-level dialogue aimed at enhancing economic relations and boosting bilateral trade and investment. Under the FSECC process, the two governments hold a regular series of working groups, including the Economic Partnership Commission (EPC) and the Trade and Investment Framework Agreement Council (TIFA), aimed at addressing specific trade and investment issues, as well as opening new areas of economic cooperation. Under the State Department-led EPC, the two sides are discussing specific steps to increase bilateral cooperation on finance, energy, innovation, and infrastructure sectors, as well as increasing cooperation in third countries. The two countries held the ninth EPC in November 2012 in Washington and will next meet in May 2013 in Ankara. The United States and Turkey have also established an FSECC Business Council, which held its first meeting in September 2011, and has suggested ways to improve bilateral business ties.

The United States and Turkey signed a Science and Technology (S&T) agreement that will deepen and diversify relations by facilitating more joint research; exchanges of scientists, researchers, and specialists; and establishment of science-based public-private partnerships. In April 2013, the inaugural meeting of the Joint S&T Commission will be held in Ankara, which will encompass working groups co-chaired by Turkish and American scientists on issues such as biomedical research, engineering for a sustainable future, education technologies, material sciences, energy research, innovative technologies in agricultural research, and natural hazards.

The United States and Turkey continue to cooperate on a range of entrepreneurship programs, including the State Department's Global Entrepreneurship Program (GEP) and the private-sector-led Partners for a New Beginning (PNB). Turkey has been a leader in both initiatives, which are aimed at supporting growth of entrepreneurship and small and medium enterprises in Turkey and the region.

Strong bilateral political relations, as well as cooperation in the region, have helped support a significant increase in U.S.-Turkey bilateral trade over the last three years. According to Turkish Statistical Institute data, trade during 2009-2012 increased approximately 70%. In 2012, bilateral trade will be lower than 2011, but Turkey continues to be one of the top six U.S. export markets and an important part of the Administration's National Export Initiative (NEI).

U.S. - Turkey bilateral trade		
Year	U.S. imports from Turkey	U.S. exports to Turkey
2009	3,240,597	8,575,737
2010	3,762,919	12,318,745
2011	4,584,029	16,034,121
2012	5,614,819	14,131,309

Source: Turkish Statistical Institute (In thousands of USD).

Openness to Foreign Investment

In 2011, the ruling Justice and Development Party (AKP) won a third term in office. As part of its election campaign, the AKP has heavily promoted its plan to become a top ten economy by 2023 (http://www.akparti.org.tr/english). In order to achieve this goal, the Government of Turkey (GOT) has developed specific strategies for 24 industrial sectors, including eight priority sectors. It has also established specific plans for physical infrastructure upgrades, as well as a major expansion of Turkey's health, information technology, and education sectors, all of which are geared to make the Turkish workforce and companies more competitive. GOT recognizes that the domestic economy alone will not be sufficient to reach these goals and that Turkey will need to attract significant new foreign direct investment (FDI).

Turkey has one of the most liberal legal regimes for FDI in Europe. In 2011, Turkey attracted USD 15.7 billion in FDI, although a significant portion of this came from portfolio investment. However, this level is still far below Turkey's potential, as well as below the levels needed for Turkey to reach its 2023 goal, and GOT is actively seeking greater U.S. FDI. In order to attract U.S. FDI, Turkey needs to increase trade advocacy and export promotion efforts, as well as access to credit, especially for small and medium-sized businesses involved in high value-added goods and services. Turkey must also better enforce international trade rules; increase engagement with foreign investors on policy issues; and pursue policies to promote strong, sustainable, and balanced growth.

According to the United Nations Conference on Trade and Development (UNCTAD) World Investment Report 2012, Turkey performed below its potential in 2011 despite the fact that it climbed six notches in its global ranking from 29th place in 2010 to 23rd place (http://www.unctad-docs.org/files/UNCTAD-Turkey). UNCTAD also ranked Turkey as the 12th most attractive destination for FDI among developing countries. A number of measures have served to increase national and foreign investors' confidence in Turkey's economy: structural reforms undertaken by GOT over the last decade, a strong banking sector, tight fiscal controls, efforts to reduce the size of the informal economy, increasing flexibility of the labor market, improving skills of workers, and continuing privatization of state economic enterprises. GOT has privatized state economic enterprises through block sales, public offerings, or a combination of both. Transactions completed under the Turkish privatization program generated USD 3 billion in 2012. GOT is committed to continuing the privatization process despite contraction in global capital flows.

With the exception of some sectors (highlighted below), areas open to the Turkish private sector are also generally open to foreign participation and investment. However, all investors – regardless of nationality – face some challenges: excessive bureaucracy, a slow judicial system, high and sometimes inconsistently applied taxes, weaknesses in corporate governance, sometimes unpredictable decisions made at the local government level, and frequent changes in the legal and regulatory environment. The Parliament amended the Law of Obligations (debt regulations), and a new Commercial Code became effective in July 2012. Major structural reforms are expected in 2013 that will create a more transparent, equal, fair, and modern investment and business environment and improve Turkey's rankings in global indices. Venture capital and angel investing is currently nascent in Turkey, but new legislation that went into effect in late 2012 will facilitate greater development of these sorts of financing opportunities.

Turkish Industrial Strategy

In January 2011, the Ministry of Science, Industry, and Technology (MSIT) announced Turkey's Industrial Strategy, which identifies 24 key areas to increase Turkey's competitiveness and productivity, and targets aimed at transforming Turkey into a technology base for manufacturing of medium- to high-technology products. MSIT has developed specific strategies and action plans for six priority sectors: iron and steel, automotive, chemicals, machinery, electrionic equipment, and ceramics. GOT additionally announced in early 2013 that medicines and medical devices are now priority sectors; MSIT is working on the pharmaceutical industry sector strategy and action plan which is expected to be released in the first half of 2013. The Industrial Strategy identifies the following areas as major potential drivers that can help increase exports and FDI, and transform Turkey into Eurasia's technology base: innovation-led productivity; increasing production of medium- and high-technology goods; increasing capital for knowledge-intensive sectors; creation of a stronger knowledge-based economy; and a developing a well-educated and highly qualified work force. (http://www.sanayi.gov.tr/Default.aspx?lng=en)

Partnerships in Improving the Investment Climate

Since 2001, GOT has pursued a comprehensive investment climate reform program aimed at streamlining investment-related procedures and attracting more FDI. The Coordination Council for the Improvement of Investment Environment (YOIKK), a national platform jointly formed by the public and private sectors, provides technical guidance for issues relating to the investment environment.

In 2004, the Investment Advisory Council of Turkey (IAC) was created to provide an international perspective for Turkey's reform agenda. IAC members include executives from multinational companies, representatives of international institutions such as the IMF, World Bank and European Investment Bank, and the heads of Turkish NGOs representing the private sector. The Council, chaired by the Prime Minister, convenes yearly to advise the Turkey Government on the direction of its reform program. The Council's recommendations serve as guidelines for the YOIKK platform, and Council recommendations are published in the Turkish Treasury's annual IAC Progress Reports.

In addition to structural reforms, Turkey's Investment Support and Promotion Agency (ISPAT), whose main objective is to support new investors throughout the business establishment process and solve problems that arise after establishment, plays an important role in facilitating a business and investment-friendly environment.

ISPAT serves as an advocate within the GOT for reforms that promote investment and works to raise both domestic and international awareness of the benefits of investment.

Investment Issues

Renewable Encrgy

GOT continues to promote investment in renewable energy production as well as equipment manufacture, with a goal to develop 20,000 megawatts (MW) of wind power, 600 MW of geothermal power, and up to 9,000 MW of solar power by 2023. Under the 2010 Renewable Energy Incentives Law, GOT offers power purchase guarantees and a feed-in tariff for electricity produced from renewable sources, but does not offer similar power purchase agreements for thermal power plants, which must sell to the spot market or through bilateral contracts. In 2012, the Ministry of Energy and Natural Resources developed implementing regulations for the Renewable Energy Incentives Law that clarified minimum local content thresholds for a product to qualify for additional feed-in tariff bonuses. The Energy Market Regulatory Authority continues to award licenses for new wind and geothermal projects and is expected to begin accepting applications for new solar power projects in June 2013.

Health Care, Transportation, and Information Technology

To meet ambitious export goals, GOT is planning significant new investment in infrastructure, including in the health care (particularly hospitals) and transportation sectors (ports, airports, and rail, light-rail, and road infrastructure). The Ministry of Health has thus far announced tenders for16 public-private partnership health campus projects all over Turkey at a cost of USD10 billion. Project agreements have been signed for three projects: the Kayseri Integrated Health Campus, Ankara Bilkent Integrated Health Campus, and the Ankara Etlik Integrated Health Campus.

Turkey plans to make significant infrastructure upgrades for ports, airports, road, and rail over the next decade. The Turkish private sector is also spear-heading projects with neighboring countries aimed at establishing an intermodal transportation network to revive the ancient Silk Road.

As part of an effort to improve Turkey's education system, GOT has embarked on a multibillion dollar project to provide Turkish students with tablet computers and schools with smart boards. The project will require expanding internet broadband throughout Turkey, as well as developing educational content and applications for tablets and smart boards. Turkey is also planning to develop greater cloud computing capacity. All these projects will provide significant opportunities for U.S. information and communication technology (ICT) companies, and the Turkish Government is actively seeking U.S. investors and partners, including for financing.

Pharmaceuticals

Turkey's pharmaceutical sector is a good example of a sector in which GOT policies complicate Turkey's ability to fully realize its development potential. Health sector reform in 2006 created a much larger pharmaceutical market dominated by Turkey's state health care system. Coupled with Turkey's young and growing population, this should have made Turkey an attractive market for pharmaceutical investment. However, two significant issues continue to inhibit innovative pharmaceutical firms' trade and investment in Turkey: a pricing/exchange rate issue and delays in obtaining GMP (Good Manufacturing Practices) inspection approvals from the Turkish Ministry of Health (MOH).

The MOH and the Turkish Ministry of Labor and Social Security (MLSS) both play important roles in pharmaceutical pricing. The MOH sets the maximum price that can be charged for medicines, and the MLSS negotiates pharmaceutical bulk prices for products that are distributed through Turkey's national health care system. In 2009 the MOH negotiated a pharmaceutical budget with industry that provided significant discounts on pharmaceutical purchases of products distributed through the Turkey's national health care system, within the context of an overall gradual increase in pharmaceutical spending each year through 2012. However, in mid 2010 and late 2011, MOH and MLSS noted budget shortfalls and requested greater discounts from companies, which they were compelled to give given GOT's dominant role in pharmaceutical spending. In December 2012, MLSS indicated to industry that the new pharmaceutical budget for 2013-2015 was almost finalized. However, new budget figures are well below industry's expectations, and GOT did not propose to provide any relief in regard to discounts or the exchange rate.

In addition to the pricing/exchange rate issues, innovative pharmaceutical firms complain about the slow pace of MOH GMP inspections. Two years ago the MOH began enforcing an existing law requiring that all companies applying to market pharmaceutical products in Turkey have a GMP certificate issued by the MOH. The MOH continues to build inspection capacity, and its inspection rate has improved. Late in December 2012, after significant appeals from industry, the Minister of Health committed to start parallel submissions, which will allow for simultaneous marketing authorization and GMP inspections – an action that will likely expedite the entry of innovative pharmaceutical into the Turkish market and help reduce the GMP backlog. MOH also committed to publishing implementation guidelines for the parallel submission process beginning in February 2013.

There is increasing awareness among GOT agencies that the pharmaceutical sector should be a strategic sector for Turkey, and the dialogue between industry and GOT officials has improved significantly over the last two years. GOT announced in early 2013 that medicines and medical devices are now priority sectors. However, despite several new investments and positive policy developments in 2012, innovative pharmaceutical companies still complain about lack of predictability and transparency in regulation making, which continues to inhibit pharmaceutical investment in Turkey.

Business Registration

Recent reforms in Turkey have simplified procedures to establish a company, reduced permit requirements, instituted a single company registration form, and enabled individuals to register their companies through local commercial registry offices of the Union of Chambers and Commodity Exchanges of Turkey (TOBB). However, according to the International Finance Corporation/World Bank 2013 'Doing Business' Report for Turkey, Turkey ranked 71 among 185 world economies, dropping three places from its 2012 ranking. According to the report, Turkey did relatively better in dealing with construction permits, registering property, enforcing contracts, and resolving insolvency compared to the previous year. Starting a business in Turkey requires a similar number of procedures as in other European countries, but it takes half the number of days, and it costs almost 140% more to start a business in Turkey. The Doing Business in Turkey report can be found at: http://www.doingbusiness.org/data/exploreeconomies/turkey/

Judicial Reforms

GOT continues to implement judicial reforms aimed at attracting foreign investment to Turkey. The National Judiciary Network project on automation and integration, overseen by the Ministry of Justice, is speeding up processing of commercial cases by facilitating document-sharing and court records, as well as allowing for filing suits online. GOT has also improved foreign investors' access to judiciary recourse, including legal aid and Alternative Dispute Resolution mechanisms supported by the U.S., the EU, and the World Bank. The Competition Authority in Turkey is an autonomous agency that plays an important role in assuring equal, fair, and transparent competition and consumer welfare-oriented market mechanisms, regardless of corporate nationality.

Taxation

In recent years, Turkish Government policies have made the taxation system more investor-friendly. In 2006, the basic corporate tax rate was reduced from 30% to 20%. GOT also cancelled the withholding tax for foreign investors' holdings of bonds, bills, and stocks - while retaining it for bank deposits and repurchase agreements. In addition, the Tax Administration established a separate unit in 2007 to handle tax collection from large corporations. Despite these improvements, GOT has not yet been able to implement further planned tax reforms, including reducing the employment tax, which is among the highest among members of the Organization for Economic Cooperation and Development (OECD).

In December 2010, the Turkish Finance Ministry announced new tax rates for capital accounts aimed at encouraging the issuance of corporate bonds with longer-term maturity. For non-domestic bonds, the withholding tax on interest is 0% for 5-year-maturity or higher bonds, 5% for bonds with 3 to 5-year maturity, and 10% for bonds with maturity less than three years. In addition, banking and insurance transactions tax applied to sale or repo transactions of domestically issued corporate bonds was reduced from 5% to 1. GOT also decreased withholding taxes on bank deposits with longer maturity aiming at attracting longer term savings.

Withholding tax on Turkish Lira time deposits with maturity longer than one year decreased to 10% from 15% while rates for the deposits up to 6 months are kept at 15%. On Foreign Currency (FX) accounts, withholding tax rate is decreased to 13% from 15% on deposits with maturity more than one year and the rate is increased to 18% for FX deposits up to six months.

The GOT is aware that between 30-50% of the economy is unregistered, which represents a competitive disadvantage for legitimate firms. Turkish industrialists anticipate that GOT will implement more tax reform in 2013 that will help to reduce the unregistered economy and broaden the tax base while also improving Turkey's competitiveness.

CURRENCY CONVERSION AND CAPITAL TRANSFER POLICIES

Turkish law guarantees the free transfer of profits, fees, and royalties, and repatriation of capital. This guarantee is reflected in Turkey's 1990 Bilateral Investment Treaty (BIT) with the United States, which mandates unrestricted and prompt transfer in a freely-usable currency at a legal market-clearing rate for all investment- related funds. There is no difficulty in obtaining foreign exchange, and there are no foreign exchange restrictions. However, foreign petroleum companies operating in Turkey complain that amendments to the Turkish Petroleum law make it difficult for foreign companies to transfer profits.

Affected companies have unsuccessfully challenged this in court. A new Petroleum Law that would alleviate this problem and improve the investment environment for oil and gas exploration is in development.

EXPROPRIATION AND COMPENSATION

Under the U.S.-Turkey BIT, expropriation can only occur in accordance with due process of law, can only be for a public purpose, and must be non-discriminatory. Compensation must be reasonably prompt, adequate, and effective. The BIT ensures U.S. investors have full access to Turkey's local courts and the ability to take the host government directly to third-party international binding arbitration to settle investment disputes. There is also a provision for state-to-state dispute settlement.

GOT occasionally expropriates private real property for public works or for state industrial projects. The GOT agency expropriating the property negotiates the purchase price. If owners of the property do not agree with the proposed price, they are able to challenge the expropriation in court and ask for additional compensation. There are no outstanding expropriation or nationalization cases.

DISPUTE SETTLEMENT

There are some outstanding investment disputes between U.S. companies and Turkish governmental bodies, particularly in the energy sector.

Turkey's legal system provides means for enforcing property and contractual rights, and there are written commercial and bankruptcy laws. However, Turkey's court system is overburdened, which sometimes results in slow decisions and judges lacking sufficient time to grasp complex issues. Judgments of foreign courts, under certain circumstances, need to be upheld by local courts before they are accepted and enforced. Monetary judgments are usually made in local currency, but there are provisions for incorporating exchange rate differentials in claims. The Turkish Government is working on judiciary reform that aims at shortening the duration of judicial proceeding and bring greater efficiency to the Turkish judiciary system through specialized courts (such as Intellectual Property Rights courts, a number of which already exist in Turkey).

Turkey is a member of the International Center for the Settlement of Investment Disputes (ICSID) and is a signatory of the New York Convention of 1958 on the Recognition and Enforcement of Foreign Arbitral Awards. Turkey ratified the Convention of the Multinational Investment Guarantee Agency (MIGA) in 1987. There are no arbitration cases involving a U.S. company pending before ICSID. The U.S.-Turkey BIT affords protection to U.S. investments in Turkey by providing certain mutual guarantees and creating a more stable and predictable legal framework for U.S. investors.

Turkish law accepts binding international arbitration of investment disputes between foreign investors and the state. In practice, however, Turkish courts have on occasion failed to uphold an international arbitration ruling involving private companies.

PERFORMANCE REQUIREMENTS/INCENTIVES

Turkey is a party to the WTO Agreement on Trade Related Investment Measures (TRIMS). Turkey's investment incentive system was substantially amended in 2006 and again in 2012 to promote investment and encourage exports. In 2009 the Turkish Parliament passed a state investment incentive decree that provides tax benefits and increased credit opportunities. It is applied in diverse ways according to the location, scale, and subject of the investment and includes exemption from customs duties and fund levies, customs, and value-added (VAT) tax exemptions for locally-purchased or imported machinery and equipment. The Turkish Treasury also covers selected parts of investment credit interest rates for SMEs, research and development projects, environmental projects, and projects in prioritized development provinces that have annual per capita income below USD 1,500.

There are no performance requirements imposed as a condition for establishing, maintaining, or expanding investment in Turkey. There are no requirements that investors purchase from local sources or export a certain percentage of output. Investors' access to foreign exchange is not conditioned on exports.

There are no requirements that nationals own shares in foreign investments, that the shares of foreign equity be reduced over time, or that the investor transfer technology on certain terms. There are no government-imposed conditions on permission to invest, including location in specific geographical areas, specific percentage of local content – for goods or services – or local equity, import substitution, export requirements or targets, technology transfer, or local financing.

GOT requirements for disclosure of proprietary information as part of the regulatory approval process are consistent with internationally accepted practices. Enterprises with foreign capital must send their activity report submitted to shareholders, their auditor's report, and their balance sheets to the Treasury's Foreign Investment Directorate every year by May.

With the exceptions noted above under "Openness to Foreign Investment" and below under "Transparency of the Regulatory System," Turkey grants all rights, incentives, exemptions, and privileges available to national businesses to foreign business on a most-favored-nation (MFN) basis. U.S. and other foreign firms can participate in government-financed and/or subsidized research and development programs on a national treatment basis.

GOT announced new incentives in 2012 that give priority to high-tech, high value-added, globally competitive sectors and put in place new regional incentive programs to reduce regional economic disparities and increase regional competitiveness. The new investment incentives involve a "tiered" system which provide for greater incentives to invest in less developed parts of the country. The map and explanation of the program can be found at: http://www.invest.gov.tr/en-US/Maps/Pages/InteractiveMap.aspx.

Turkish law and regulations affecting the investment climate continue to evolve. Potential investors should check with appropriate Turkish government sources for current detailed information. ISPAT's web site provides the text of regulations governing foreign investment and incentives, as well as other useful background information: www.invest.gov.tr.

Offsets are an important aspect of Turkey's military procurement, and offset guidelines have been modified to encourage direct investment and technology transfer.

ENTREPRENEURSHIP

Turkey pays close attention to the impact microeconomic factors have on business development and growth and is seeking to foster entrepreneurship and small and medium-sized enterprises (SMEs). Through the Small and Medium Enterprises Development Organization (KOSGEB), the Turkish Government provides various incentives for innovative ideas and cutting edge technologies, in addition to providing SMEs easier access to medium and long-term funds. There is also a number of technology development zones (TDZs) in Turkey where entreprenuers are given assistance in commercializing business ideas.

GOT provides support to TDZs, including infrastructure and facilities; exemption from income and corporate taxes for profits derived from software and R&D activities (through December 2013); exemption from all taxes for the wages of researchers, software, and R&D personnel employed within the TDZ (through December 2013); value-added tax (VAT) and corporate tax exemptions for IT specific sectors; and customs and duties exemptions.

Turkey's Scientific and Technological Research Council (TUBITAK) has special programs for entrepreneurs in the technology sector, and the Turkish Technology Development Foundation (TTGV) has programs that provide capital loans for R&D projects and/or cover R&D-related expenses. Projects eligible for such incentives include concept development, technological research, technical feasibility research, laboratory studies to transform concept into design, design and sketching studies, prototype production, construction of pilot facilities, test production, patent and license studies, and activities related to post-scale problems stemming from product design. In November 2012, TUBITAK announced a Technology Transfer Office Support Program, which will provide USD 1 million in grants to establish Technology Transfer Offices (TTOs) in Turkey.

Right to Private Ownership and Establishment

Foreign-owned interests in the petroleum, mining, broadcasting, maritime transportation, and aviation sectors are subject to special regulatory requirements. In broadcasting, equity participation of foreign shareholders is restricted to 25%. Foreign equity participation in the aviation and maritime transportation sectors is 49%.

With the exceptions noted above, private entities may freely establish, acquire, and dispose of interests in business enterprises, and foreign participation is permitted up to 100%. Turkey has an independent Competition Board. With respect to access to markets, credit, and other business operations, competitive equality is the standard applied to private enterprises that seek to compete with public enterprises. Regulations governing foreign investment in Turkey are, in general, transparent. In most sectors Turkey does not have an investment screening system for foreign investors; only notification is required.

The Ministry of Environment and Urbanization completed a new draft law on title deed registration in 2012. This law abandoned the former requirement that foreign purchasers of real estate in Turkey had to be in partnership with a Turkish individual or company that owns at least a 50% share in the property and is much more flexible in allowing international companies to purchase real property. The new law also increases the upper limit on real estate purchases by foreign individuals to 30 hectares and allows further increases up to 60 hectares with permission from the Council of Ministers.

Protection of Property Rights

Secured interests in property, both movable and real, are recognized and enforced, and there is a reliable system of recording such security interests. For example, there is a land registry office where real estate is registered. Turkey's legal system protects and facilitates acquisition and disposal of property rights, including land, buildings, and mortgages, although some parties have complained that the courts are slow to render decisions and are susceptible to external influence (see "Dispute Settlement").

Turkey is signatory to a number of international conventions, including the Stockholm Act of the Paris Convention, the Patent Cooperation Treaty, and the Strasbourg Agreement. In 2008, Turkey acceded to the WIPO

Copyright Treaty and Performances and Phonograms Treaty. Turkey accepts patent applications in compliance with the TRIPS agreement "mailbox" provisions.

Turkey's intellectual property rights regime has improved in recent years, but deficiencies remain. In 2008, Turkey was on the U.S. Special 301 Priority Watch List. In 2009 it was upgraded to the U.S. Special 301 Watch List, where it remained in 2010, 2011, and 2012. Although there has been increased IPR enforcement actions and successful public awareness campaigns, piracy and counterfeiting remain serious problems. There is widespread and often sophisticated counterfeiting of trademarked items, especially apparel. Business software and online music piracy are increasing, and book and entertainment software piracy remain areas of concern.

Turkey has not yet completed legislative reforms needed to ensure effective IPR protection and enforcement. Delays in the judicial and legislative processes contribute to deficiencies in the overall IPR protection and enforcement regime. Turkey's copyright law, as amended in 2004, provides deterrent penalties for copyright infringement. The law contains several strong anti-piracy provisions, including a ban on street sales of all copyrighted products and authorization for law enforcement authorities to take action without a complaint by the rights holder. In 2012, the Turkish Ministry of Culture and Tourism drafted amendments to Turkey's copyright law and undertook a lengthy process of soliciting stakeholder opinions, including other GOT agencies and 40 different collecting societies. These amendments are currently awaiting approval by the Turkish Prime Ministry. After Prime Ministry approval, the amendments will be submitted to the Turkish Parliament for ratification.

Turkey's patent law has been in force since 1995 and was amended in 2004. Patents are granted for 20 years to any invention in any field of technology which is novel, involves an inventive step, and has industrial applications. In 2012, the Turkish Patent Institute (TPI) completed a new draft patent law, which we expect will come before the Turkish Parliament in 2013.

The United States has a Copyright Working Group and the EU has an IPR Working Group with GOT to address intellectual property related issues and exchange views on developing more efficient and effective IPR enforcement.

In general, the Turkish Ministry of Health provides protection for confidential test data submitted in support of applications to market pharmaceutical products. However, several provisions undermine protection for confidential test data. Due to the relatively short six-year data-exclusivity period and delays by the Turkish MOH in granting Good Manufacturing

Practice inspection certificates and marketing approvals, pharmaceutical data protection remains a concern, particularly for innovative products. In addition, Turkey's patent law does not contain interim protection for pharmaceuticals in the research and development pipeline. Research-based pharmaceutical companies have criticized patent provisions which delay the initiation of infringement suits until after the patent is approved and published, permit use of a patented invention to generate data needed for the marketing approval of generic pharmaceutical products, and give judges wider discretion over penalties in infringement cases.

Trademark holders also note that Turkey provides protection for commercial seed under its Plant Variety Protection (PVP) Law.

Turkish intellectual property (IP) law allows both civil and criminal actions. In general, civil actions include requests for determination of infringement, cessation of acts of infringement, seizure of counterfeit goods, and compensation of damages. Criminal actions include imprisonment, pecuniary punishment, closure of job sites, and prohibition from commerce.

Turkey has specialized intellectual property IP courts, presided over by judges who have had training in intellectual property law, in Istanbul, Ankara, and Izmir. IP litigation in Turkey generally begins in these courts and moves to the Supreme Court if an appeal is filed. If the alleged offense does not occur in Istanbul, Ankara or Izmir, the case begins in civil courts that act as IP courts.

The Seventh Global Congress on Combating Counterfeiting and Piracy will be held in Istanbul in April 2013 under the auspices of Turkish Ministry of Customs and Trade. The Congress aims to build cooperation between countries to enhance public awareness, develop concerted action to confront problems arising from counterfeiting and piracy, and find sustainable solutions to stop trade in IPR-infringing goods.

Further information on the intellectual property situation in Turkey is available in the U.S. National Trade Estimate and Special 301 reports, available under the "reports" tab on the U.S. Trade Representative's website: www.ustr.gov.

Transparency of the Regulatory System

GOT has adopted policies and laws that in principle should foster competition and transparency. However, foreign companies in several sectors claim that regulations are sometimes applied in a nontransparent manner.

Turkey is an observer to the WTO Government Procurement Agreement. Turkish legislation generally requires competitive bidding procedures in the public sector. A Public Procurement board exists to oversee public tenders, and there are minimum bidding thresholds under which foreign companies are prohibited from bidding on public tenders. The law gives preference to domestic bidders, Turkish citizens, and legal entities established by them, as well as to corporate entities established under Turkish law by foreign companies. The public procurement law has been amended eight times since its enactment and has been cited by the EU as not being in conformity with the EU *acquis communautaire*.

In general, labor, health and safety laws and policies do not distort or impede investment, although legal restrictions on discharging employees may provide a disincentive to labor-intensive activity in the formal economy. Generous tax preferences for free zones have provided a stimulus to investment in these zones. Similarly, incentives for investment in certain low-income provinces appear to be stimulating investment there (see "Performance Requirements/Incentives").

Efficient Capital Markets and Portfolio Investment

GOT has taken a number of important steps in recent years to strengthen and better regulate the banking system. A 2005 revision of the Banking Law brought tighter bank regulation, notably by broadening the range of expertise inspectors can draw on when conducting on-site inspections. GOT adopted a new Capital Markets Law in 2012, which will bring about greater corporate accountability, protection of minority share-holders, and financial statement transparency.

As of January 2013, there are 26 deposit-taking commercial banks and 13 development and investment banks operating in Turkey. Sector assets as of September 2012 totaled approximately USD 690 billion according to data from the Banks' Association of Turkey. Total loans for the banking sector totaled USD 404.3 billion for the same period. The independent Banking and Regulation Supervision Agency (BRSA) monitors and supervises Turkey's banks. The BRSA is headed by a board whose seven members are appointed for six-year terms. In addition, bank deposits are protected by an independent deposit insurance agency, the State Deposit Insurance Fund (SDIF).

Because of historically high local borrowing costs and short repayment periods, foreign and local firms have frequently sought credit from international markets to finance their activities. In November 2012, Fitch Ratings upgraded Turkey to investment grade for the first time in almost two decades (since 1994), citing a moderating debt burden, healthy banking system, and sound economic management. With investors increasingly viewing Turkey as a strong emerging economy, Turkey's risk premium has begun to decrease, while accessibility to medium and long-term financing at lower costs has increased. However, growing economic problems in Europe are expected to continue to impede external financing in 2013.

The Istanbul Stock Exchange (ISE), formed in 1985, is becoming a significant emerging market stock exchange. Although Turkey must further develop its capital markets, the 2012 Capital Markets Law allowed ISE to expand to include the Istanbul Gold Exchange Market and the Futures Contract Market. As of October 2012, 402 companies were listed on the exchange with total market capitalization of USD 269 billion. The Capital Markets Board is responsible for overseeing activities, including activities of ISE-quoted companies and securities and investment houses. The Turkish private sector continues to be dominated by a number of large holding companies, many of which are family-owned, and most large businesses continue to float publicly only a minority portion of shares in order to limit outside interference in company management. There has been no recent hostile takeover attempt by either international or domestic parties. Capital market instruments are still developing in Turkey. Turkey's first mortgage law was adopted in 2007. Venture capital and hedging instruments are also currently very limited, but a new law came into effect in 2012 that will increase financing opportunities through venture capital and angel investing.

Political Violence

Terrorist groups operating in Turkey include the Kurdish separatists and Marxist-Leninists, as well as Al-Qa'ida and its affiliates.

The Revolutionary People's Liberation Party/Front (DHKP/C) is a virulent Marxist-Leninist group with anti-U.S. and anti-NATO views and which has been designated by the United States as a terrorist since 1997. On February 1, 2013 a DHKP/C suicide bomber attacked U.S. Embassy Ankara at a security-check entrance, killing one security guard and seriously injuring a Turkish journalist. A DKHP/C suicide bomber also attacked a police station

Istanbul on September 11, 2012, killing one police officer and injuring seven bystanders.

Most prominent among the terrorist groups operating in Turkey is Kongra-Gel (KGK, also known as the Kurdistan Workers' Party or PKK). Composed primarily of ethnic Kurds with a separatist agenda, the PKK has historically operated from areas in southeastern Turkey and northern Iraq and targeted mainly Turkish security forces. After a calmer 2011, due in part to a cease-fire in the lead-up to national elections in June 2011, the rate of PKK terror attacks and Turkish military operations to counter them increased significantly in 2012. Typical tactics included roadside checkpoints forcing vehicles to stop, kidnapping of political figures and teachers (although most victims were returned in a few days), ambushes of military patrols in the countryside, improvised explosive devices along known military or police routes, and bombings of both security and civilian targets in urban areas (nearly all in the southeastern part of Turkey). At the end of 2012, GOT revealed that it was in private talks with imprisoned PKK leader Abdullah Ocalan, aimed at a possible political settlement of the PKK armed conflict.

For the latest security information on Turkey and other countries, see http://travel.state, where current Worldwide Caution Public Announcements, Travel Warnings, and Public Announcements can be found.

Corruption

Corruption is somewhat of a problem in Turkey. Parliament continues to probe corruption allegations involving senior officials in previous governments, particularly in connection with energy projects. The judicial system is also perceived to be susceptible to external influence and to be biased against outsiders to some degree.

Public procurement reforms were designed to make procurement more transparent and less susceptible to political interference, including through the establishment of an independent public procurement board with the power to void contracts. Turkey is not yet a signatory to the WTO Government Procurement Agreement (GPA), although it has maintained observer status for over a decade.

Turkish legislation outlaws bribery, and some prosecutions of government officials for corruption have taken place. However, enforcement is uneven. Turkey ratified the OECD Convention on Combating Bribery of Public Officials and passed implementing legislation in January 2003 to provide that bribes of foreign officials, as well as domestic, are illegal. In 2006, Turkey's Parliament ratified the UN Convention against Corruption.

Turkey's Criminal Code makes it unlawful to promise or to give any advantage to foreign government officials in exchange for their assistance in providing improper advantage in the conduct of international business. In the event that such a crime makes an unlawful benefit to a legal entity, such legal entity shall be subject to certain security measures. The provisions of the Criminal Law regarding bribing of foreign governmental officials are in line with the provisions of the Foreign Corrupt Practices Act of 1977 of the United States (FCPA).

There are, however, a number of differences between Turkish law and the FCPA. For example, there is not an exception under Turkish law for payments to facilitate or expedite performance of a "routine governmental action" in terms of the FCPA. Another difference is that the FCPA does not provide for punishment by imprisonment, while the Turkish law provides for punishment by imprisonment from 4 to 12 years. The Prime Ministry's Inspection Board, which advises the Corruption Investigations Committee, is responsible for investigating major corruption cases brought to its attention by the Committee. Nearly every state agency has its own inspector corps responsible for investigating internal corruption. The Parliament can establish investigative commissions to examine corruption allegations concerning cabinet ministers; a majority vote is needed to send these cases to the Supreme Court for further action.

According to Transparency International's (TI) annual Corruption Perception Index Data, Turkey moved from 61st to 54th in TI's ranking of 176 countries and territories among the world in 2012 (see http://www.transparency.org/cpi2012/results). Transparency International has an affiliated NGO in Istanbul.

Bilateral Investment Agreements

Since 1962, Turkey has been negotiating and signing agreements for the reciprocal promotion and protection of investments. As of January 1, 2013, Turkey had 75 bilateral investment agreements in force with: Afghanistan, Albania, Argentina, Austria, Australia, Azerbaijan, Bangladesh, Belarus, Belgium, Bosnia and Herzegovina, Bulgaria, China, Croatia, Cuba, Czech Republic, Denmark, Egypt, Estonia, Ethiopia, Finland, France, Georgia, Germany, Greece, Hungary, India, Indonesia, Iran, Israel, Italy, Japan, Jordan,

Kazakhstan, Kuwait, Kyrgyzstan, Latvia, Lebanon, Libya, Lithuania, Luxembourg, Macedonia, Malaysia, Malta, Moldova, Mongolia, Morocco, Netherlands, Oman, Saudi Arabia, Pakistan, Philippines, Poland, Portugal, Qatar, Romania, Russian Federation, Serbia, Singapore, Slovakia, Slovenia, South Korea, Spain, Sweden, Switzerland, Syria, Tajikistan, Thailand, Tunisia, Turkmenistan, United Arab Emirates, United Kingdom, United States, Ukraine, Uzbekistan, and Yemen.

OPIC and Other Investment Insurance Programs

The Overseas Private Investment Corporation (OPIC) offers a full range of programs in Turkey, including political risk insurance for U.S. investors, under its bilateral agreement with Turkey. OPIC is also active in financing private investment projects implemented by U.S. investors in Turkey. OPIC-supported direct equity funds, including the USD 200 million Soros Private Equity Fund, can make direct equity investments in private sector projects in Turkey. Currently, OPIC is looking to support increased lending for renewable energy and energy efficiency projects in Turkey. Small and medium-sized U.S. investors in Turkey are also eligible to utilize the Small Business Center facility at OPIC, offering OPIC finance and insurance support on an expedited basis for loans from USD 100,000 to USD 10 million. In 1987, Turkey became a member of the Multinational Investment Guarantee Agency (MIGA).

Labor

Turkey has a population of 75.6 million, with 30% under the age of 14. Over 76% of the Turkish population lives in urban areas. The Turkish labor force numbers 26.8 million, of which 24.3 million are employed. Approximately 26.2% of the workforce works in agriculture; 19% works in industrial sector. The official unemployment rate was 9.1% as of September 2012, with 18% youth unemployment (15-24 years old). Students are required to complete eight years of schooling and remain in school until they are 15 years old. 98.17% of Turkey's population completes primary school; 36% of those who complete primary school get vocational or higher education.

Turkey has an abundance of unskilled and semi-skilled labor, and Turkey's labor force has a reputation for being hardworking, productive, and dependable. Vocational training schools exist at the high school level. Some formal apprenticeship programs remain, but informal training in traditional occupations is decreasing rapidly. Although the Ministry of Education launched projects within the framework of EU programs to meet the needs of high-tech industries - which has increased the number of qualified high-tech workers in recent years - there remains a shortage. Individual high-tech firms, both local and foreign-owned, typically conduct their own training programs. The Ministry of Science, Industry, and Technology has launched a program with TOBB to provide skilled laborers to meet manufacturing sector needs. Turkey has also undertaken a significant expansion of university programs, building dozens of new colleges and universities over the last decade to increase the skills and competitiveness of its workforce. GOT has also initiated the FATİH project that will expand internet coverage to all Turkish schools, equip Turkish classrooms with interactive smart boards, and provide students with tablet PCs.

Labor unions report their relations with management of Turkish companies is often adversarial. Employers are obliged by law to negotiate in good faith with unions that have been certified as bargaining agents. Strikes are usually of short duration and almost always peaceful. The law prohibits discrimination on the basis of union membership. While exact unionization rates are not available, they are low - a percentage probably in the single digits. There is no obligation for a worker to become a member of a union, and there is no obligation to make a collective labor agreement for any sector. However, in order to be covered by a collective labor agreement, a worker must be a member of a union. Historically, in order to be a bargaining agent, a union must have membership of more than forty percent of the workers employed in a work place and include at least three percent of the workers employed in that specific work branch. Turkish labor law mandates that a series of steps be followed - including mediation by an Arbitration Board - before a union may initiate a strike.

In October 2012, the Turkish Parliament approved the "Unions and Collective Bargaining Law," which revised regulations on trade union formation and collective bargaining. The new law lowers two thresholds for a labor union to be authorized as an agent of collective bargaining. The first relates to any given work place: where previously the union had to represent 50 percent plus one of a firm's employees, the share is now 40 percent. The second measure relates to a nationwide industry branch: where a bona fide union was previously required to have membership of at least 10 percent of workers in its sector, the new rate has been lowered to one percent from

January 1, 2013 through June 30, 2016; two percent from July 1, 2016 to June 30, 2018; and three percent after July 1, 2018.

Turkey's Economic and Social Council was established by law in 2001, headed by the Prime Minister. The Council aims to maintain an effective dialogue between the state and social parties to encourage compromise in industrial relations. It is composed of representatives from governmental bodies, labor and employer confederations, employee associations, and chambers of commerce and industry.

Turkey has signed many International Labor Organization (ILO) conventions protecting workers' rights, including conventions on Freedom of Association and Protection of the Right to Organize; Rights to Organize and to Bargain Collectively; Abolition of Forced Labor; Minimum Wage; Occupational Health and Safety; Termination of Employment; and Elimination of the Worst Forms of Child Labor. Since 1980, Turkey has faced criticism by the ILO, particularly for shortcomings in enforcement of ILO Convention 87 (Convention Concerning Freedom of Association and Protection of the Right to Organize) and Convention 98 (Convention Concerning the Application of the Principles of the Right to Organize and to Bargain Collectively).

GOT maintains a number of restrictions on the right of association and the right to strike. Civil servants (defined broadly as all employees of central government ministries, including teachers) are allowed to form trade unions and to engage in limited collective negotiations, but are prohibited from striking. Certain vital public employees, such as military and police, cannot form unions. According to the new Unions Law, the list of sectors barred from striking has also been expanded to: life or property rescuing; funeral and mortuary work; production; refining/distillation; distribution of city water; electricity; natural gas and oil; petrochemical works, including with naphtha and natural gas; work places directly run by Defense Ministry, Gendarmerie, and Coast Guard; banking and public notaries; hospitals; firefighting; land, sea, railway service; and all urban public transportation. (Aviation is not included.)

The EU's October 2012 Progress Report underscores that Turkey's 2012 amended legislation on collective bargaining by civil servants "is not fully in line with the EU *acquis* and ILO conventions, especially with regard to the right to strike for public servants, the process of collective bargaining and dispute settlement, as well as restrictions on large categories of public servants to form and join trade unions."

Foreign Trade Zones/Free Ports

Firms operating in Turkey's free zones have historically enjoyed many advantages.

The zones are open to a wide range of activities, including manufacturing, storage, packaging, trading, banking, and insurance. Foreign products enter and leave the free zones without payment of customs or duties. Income generated in the zones is exempt from corporate and individual income taxation and from the value-added tax, but firms are required to make social security contributions for their employees.

Additionally, standardization regulations in Turkey do not apply to the activities in the free zones, unless the products are imported into Turkey.

Sales to the Turkish domestic market are allowed, with goods and revenues transported from the zones into Turkey subject to all relevant import regulations. There are no restrictions on foreign firm operating in the free zones.

Taxpayers who possessed an operating license as of February 6, 2004, do not have to pay income or corporate tax on their earnings in free zones for the duration of their license.

Earnings based on sale of goods manufactured in free zones is exempt from income and corporate tax until the end of the year in which Turkey becomes a member of the European Union.

Earnings secured in a free zone under corporate tax immunity and paid as dividends to real person shareholders in Turkey, or to real person or legal-entity shareholders abroad, are subject to 10% withholding tax.

The tax immunity of the wage and salary income earned by persons employed in the zones by taxpayers possessing an operating license expired on December 31, 2008, except for producers that export more than 85% of their products.

GOT passed a law in November 2008, according to which producers' immunities from income and corporate tax and taxes on wage income earned in free zones were extended to coincide with Turkey's membership in the European Union.

More information can be found on the Ministry of Economy's website: www.ekonomi.gov.tr.

FOREIGN DIRECT INVESTMENT (FDI) STATISTICS

According to Central Bank of Turkey data, FDI inflows to Turkey in 2007 of USD 22 billion decreased by 12% in 2008 to USD 19.5 billion and plummeted by 57% in 2009 to USD 8.4 billion, due largely to the negative impact of the global financial crisis on investment flows worldwide. In 2010, FDI inflows began to rebound - increasing by almost 11% over 2009 to USD 9.1 billion - and continued to grow in 2011 - reaching USD 16.04 billion. During the first eleven months of 2012, FDI reached USD 11.3 billion, of which USD 8.5 billion represented net foreign capital inflows, USD 2.3 billion represented real estate purchases by foreigners, and USD 446 million represented intra-company loans.

In the January-November 2012 period, EU countries accounted for 75% of FDI capital inflow to Turkey, as compared to 85.8% in 2011; Asian and Gulf countries accounted for 14.9%, as compared to 5.4% in 2011; U.S. companies accounted for 3.9%, as compared to 5.5% in 2011; European countries other than the EU accounted for 5.3%, as compared to 2.7% in 2011; Canada accounted for 0.2%, as compared to 0.15 % in 2011, and Central and South American and Caribbean countries accounted for 0.2%, as compared to 0.48% in 2011.

In the first eleven months of 2012, according to the Central Bank of Turkey, breakdown of FDI inflows into Turkey's manufacturing industry were:

- food products, beverages and tobacco 23.8%
- electrical and optical equipment 1.8%
- chemical products 5.2%
- textiles and textile products 4.1%
- transport equipment 1.2%
- other 9.5%

FDI inflows by year *USD million*	2008	2009	2010	2011	2012 (Jan-Nov)
FDI Total (Net)	19.504	8.411	9.038	16.049	11.336
Equity Investment (Net)	14.712	6.170	6.258	13.712	8.549
Inflows	14.747	6.252	6.238	16.057	8.924
Outflows	-35	-82	-35	-1.991	-375
Intra Company Loans	1.855	459	341	-30	446
Real Estate (Net)	2.937	1.782	2.494	2.013	2.341

Central Bank of Turkey.

FDI inflows by country/region *USD million*	2008	2009	2010	2011	2012 (Jan-Nov)
European Union	11.076	4.928	4.719	11.462	6.712
Germany	1.237	498	597	665	462
Austria	586	1.019	1.584	2.419	1.399
France	679	617	623	999	92
Netherlands	1.343	718	486	1.424	1.090
U.K.	1.335	350	245	905	1.992
Italy	249	314	25	111	161
Other EU Countries	5.647	1.412	1.159	4.939	1.516
Other European Countries (excluding EU)	291	306	201	1.093	480
African Countries	82	2	0	0	0
U.S.A.	868	260	323	1.402	346
Canada	23	52	55	21	26
Central-South America and Caribbean	60	19	7	61	18
Asia	2.345	673	928	2.011	1.334
Near and Middle Eastern Countries	2.184	361	473	1.516	890
Gulf Countries	1.963	209	38	196	236
Other Near and Middle Eastern Countries	96	78	45	1.316	654
Other Asian Countries	161	312	455	495	444
Other countries	2	12	5	7	8
TOTAL	14.747	6.252	6.238	16.057	8.924

Central Bank of Turkey.

INDEX

#

20th century, 5

A

access, 5, 7, 8, 9, 18, 19, 24, 38, 43, 66, 70, 73, 84, 90, 91, 93, 94, 95
accessibility, 99
accountability, 24, 98
accounting, 20, 21, 41, 70, 72, 75
accounting standards, 70, 72, 75
acquis communautaire, 98
acquisitions, 56, 65, 73
adjustment, 72
advocacy, 84
aerospace, 2
Afghanistan, 101
Africa, 82
age, 27, 68, 102
agencies, 12, 14, 15, 19, 23, 24, 41, 46, 57, 72, 77, 89, 96
aging population, 55
agriculture, 43, 67, 102
airports, 9, 39, 87
Albania, 101
Algeria, 46
Alternative Dispute Resolution, 90
appetite, 74
appointments, 44
arbitration, 4, 10, 36, 57, 63, 91, 92
Argentina, 25, 46, 101
armed conflict, 100
arrest, 11
ASEAN, 47, 50, 51, 52
Asia, 76, 77, 107
Asia Pacific Economic Cooperation, 77
Asian countries, 47
assessment, 26
assessments, vii
assets, 17, 18, 21, 42, 43, 64, 72, 74, 75, 76, 98
Attorney General, 14, 24, 26, 45, 46
audit, 71
audits, 20
Austria, 25, 101, 107
authenticity, 15
authorities, 19, 32, 66, 76, 96
authority, 17, 33, 36, 48, 62, 75
automation, 89
automobiles, 2, 39
awareness, 25, 45, 75, 86, 89
Azerbaijan, 101

B

background information, 94
balance of payments, 49, 73

balance sheet, 20, 93
ban, 6, 96
Bangladesh, 46, 101
bank financing, 18
bank ownership, 42
banking, 16, 17, 18, 37, 42, 43, 49, 60, 72, 73, 82, 85, 90, 98, 99, 104, 105
banking sector, 16, 17, 42, 43, 73, 85, 98
bankruptcies, 63
bankruptcy, 8, 17, 36, 39, 74, 92
banks, 17, 18, 34, 42, 43, 60, 70, 72, 73, 98
bargaining, 67, 103, 104
barriers, vii, 4, 47
base, 82, 85
basis points, 74
beef, 59
beer, 4
Belarus, 25, 101
Belgium, 25, 46, 101
benefits, 12, 16, 27, 41, 43, 78, 86, 92
beverages, 106
BI, 34, 42, 43, 48, 49
bilateral, 25, 46, 77, 91, 101
bilingual, 2, 4
biotechnology, 78
board members, 71
Bolivia, 25
bond market, 43, 74
bonds, 19, 21, 42, 43, 90
bonuses, 87
borrowers, 34, 62
Bosnia, 101
Brazil, 3, 18, 25
breakdown, 106
bribes, 16, 76, 101
broadcasting, 4, 7, 59, 95
Bulgaria, 46, 101
bureaucracy, 16, 41, 85
business environment, 61, 78, 85
business model, 18
businesses, 2, 16, 18, 23, 25, 32, 37, 38, 39, 41, 56, 63, 69, 84, 93, 99
buyers, 74

C

Cabinet, 83
CAD, 82
Cambodia, 46
campaigns, 96
candidates, 27
capital account, 90
capital controls, 11
capital flows, 49, 85
capital goods, 34, 49
capital inflow, 50, 56, 106
capital markets, 18, 37, 43, 55, 73, 99
capital outflow, 73
Caribbean, 106, 107
Caribbean countries, 106
cash, 10, 24, 26, 34, 78
categorization, 50
cattle, 59
central bank, 18
certificate, 39, 68, 88
challenges, 8, 41, 45, 66, 71, 85
challenging, 36
chemical, 39, 106
chemicals, 85
children, 27, 68
Chile, 2, 25, 46, 47
China, 3, 25, 27, 47, 50, 51, 52, 79, 101
circumvent, 41
cities, 82
citizens, 8, 23, 48
City, 2, 22, 27, 78
civil action, 97
civil law, 36
civil servants, 77, 104
civil society, 25, 46
claimants, 8
classes, 44
clearinghouse, 9
clients, 24, 63
climate, vii, 15, 56, 57, 86, 93

closure, 97
clusters, 78
coal, 39
Coast Guard, 104
codes, 46
collateral, 16, 17
collective bargaining, 68, 103, 104
colleges, 103
Colombia, 2, 25
commerce, 97, 104
commercial, 11, 18, 36, 40, 43, 60, 63, 73, 74, 78, 83, 89, 90, 92, 97, 98
commercial bank, 43, 60, 73, 74, 98
commercial ties, 18, 83
communication, 88
communities, 23
community, 11, 23, 44, 45
compensation, 10, 34, 35, 40, 62, 75, 91, 97
competition, 4, 7, 17, 18, 27, 65, 70, 90, 97
competitiveness, 1, 4, 12, 48, 55, 72, 85, 91, 93, 103
competitors, 48
compliance, 37, 41, 46, 96
composition, 14, 17
computing, 88
conflict, 45, 74
conformity, 98
conglomerates, 56
congress, 15, 24
Congress, 4, 5, 6, 9, 10, 17, 23, 24, 25, 26, 97
consolidation, 43
Constitution, 19, 21, 40
constitutional amendment, 5
construction, 5, 6, 20, 32, 43, 49, 67, 74, 89, 94
consulting, 20
consumers, 17, 20
contraction, 85
control measures, 73
controlling, 17, 19, 32, 71
convention, 24
cooperation, 83, 97
coordination, 20, 31, 32
copyright, 14, 40, 41, 65, 66, 96
copyright law, 65, 96
corporate crime, 35
corporate governance, 57, 69, 70, 85
Corporate Social Responsibility, 22, 44, 75
Corporate Social Responsibility (CSR), 22, 44
corruption, 16, 24, 31, 37, 41, 44, 46, 61, 76, 77, 100, 101
cosmetics, 39
cost, 7, 9, 35, 48, 69, 87
cost of living, 69
Costa Rica, 25
cotton, 36
Council of Ministers, 95
counsel, 11, 63
counterfeiting, 14, 65, 96, 97
counterterrorism, 45
covering, 4
credit rating, 18, 19
creditors, 17, 37
crimes, 26
criticism, 104
Croatia, 46, 101
crops, 60
cross-ownership, 65
Cuba, 25, 46, 101
culture, 23, 70
currency, 26, 34, 37, 47, 61, 62, 63, 73, 91, 92
customers, 20, 34
Customs Service, 14
Czech Republic, 25, 46, 101

D

Daewoo, 74
damages, 10, 67, 97
deaths, 45

debts, 17, 62
decentralization, 12, 40, 41
decision makers, 6
defendants, 11
deficiencies, 69, 96
democratization, 56
demonstrations, 22, 45
Denmark, 25, 46, 101
deposit accounts, 62
deposits, 26, 90, 98
depreciation, 11
derivatives, 34, 39
developing countries, 85
development banks, 18
direct investment, 37, 44, 94
directors, 20, 44, 71, 73, 75
disability, 27
disappointment, 48
disclosure, 70, 93
discrimination, 26, 38, 69, 103
distillation, 104
distortions, vii
distribution, 3, 5, 19, 27, 59, 60, 104
domestic, 4, 7, 9, 11, 13, 17, 18, 21, 22, 31, 32, 34, 35, 36, 37, 38, 39, 41, 42, 43, 44, 47, 49, 56, 62, 63, 65, 67, 71, 73, 75, 84, 86, 98, 99, 101, 105
domestic demand, 31
domestic economy, 84
domestic markets, 18, 44
Dominican Republic, 25
DOT, 8
doubled, 81
draft, 7, 41, 95, 96
drawing, 63
drug smuggling, 22
due process, 91
dumping, 23
duopoly, 7

E

earnings, 34, 69, 105
economic cooperation, 83
economic development, 12, 44
economic downturn, 55, 74
economic growth, 31, 44, 74, 82
economic problem, 99
economic reform, 1, 81
economic reforms, 1, 81
economic relations, 83
education, 48, 68, 76, 79, 83, 84, 87
Egypt, 46, 47, 101
El Salvador, 25
election, 58, 84
electricity, 3, 4, 5, 19, 59, 87, 104
emergency, 15, 39, 62
emerging markets, 1, 26
employees, 16, 17, 39, 48, 75, 98, 103, 104, 105
employers, 27, 67, 68
employment, 4, 67, 68, 90
energy, 3, 4, 5, 19, 39, 43, 74, 75, 81, 83, 92, 100, 102
energy efficiency, 102
enforcement, 4, 14, 40, 45, 65, 66, 67, 96, 100, 104
engineering, 6, 83
enhancing, 16, 57, 83
entrepreneurs, 94
entrepreneurship, 83, 94
environment, 9, 17, 18, 20, 44, 61, 65, 71, 78, 85, 86, 91
environmental impact, 44, 75
EPC, 83
EPS, 67
equality, 95
equipment, 5, 23, 37, 38, 49, 72, 85, 87, 93, 106
equity, 26, 32, 35, 38, 44, 50, 93, 95, 102
Estonia, 101
ethics, 46
EU, 56, 58, 65, 79, 82, 90, 96, 98, 103, 104, 106, 107
Eurasia, 86
Europe, 50, 51, 84, 99

European Investment Bank, 86
European Union, 25, 51, 52, 105, 107
evidence, 11, 40
evolution, 70
exchange rate, 9, 48, 73, 88, 92
exclusion, 47
exercise, 7, 68
Expatriates, 37
expertise, 98
export market, 82, 84
export promotion, 84
exporter, 5
exporters, 34, 36
exports, 2, 72, 82, 86, 92, 93
exposure, 70
expropriation, 10, 34, 35, 47, 62, 91
external financing, 99
external shocks, 56
extraction, 37, 44

F

facilitate, 10, 12, 85, 101
fair market, 10, 40, 62
faith, 103
families, 70, 79
FDI, 1, 2, 3, 6, 28, 31, 46, 49, 50, 51, 52, 56, 57, 58, 79, 84, 85, 86, 106, 107
FDI inflow, 106
fear, 70
fears, 7
federal authorities, 14
federal government, 11, 16
federal law, 9, 15, 24
Federal Reserve, 9
FETA, 61, 62
financial, 4, 8, 9, 12, 16, 17, 18, 20, 26, 49, 55, 56, 57, 60, 62, 64, 69, 70, 72, 73, 74, 75, 77, 98, 106
financial firms, 73
financial intermediaries, 18
financial markets, 69, 70, 73
financial reports, 20
financial sector, 18
financial stability, 16
financial support, 64
financial system, 26
Finland, 25, 46, 101
fish, 39
fishing, 43, 59
flexibility, 85
flights, 8
flour, 39
fluctuations, 73
food, 39, 58, 60, 106
food products, 106
footwear, 12, 39
force, 26, 57, 77, 86, 96, 101
foreign assistance, 55
foreign banks, 60
foreign companies, 5, 22, 32, 37, 49, 68, 91, 97, 98
foreign direct investment, 1, 2, 56, 57, 65, 84
foreign exchange, 9, 34, 60, 73, 91, 93
foreign firms, 15, 38, 70, 93
foreign investment, 3, 4, 9, 33, 35, 41, 55, 56, 57, 58, 60, 62, 64, 70, 73, 76, 78, 89, 93, 94, 95
formation, 67, 103
France, 25, 28, 47, 101, 107
fraud, 36
free trade, 25, 27, 49, 79
freedom, 24, 48
full capacity, 24
funds, 4, 17, 18, 26, 34, 61, 62, 65, 73, 91, 94, 102

G

gambling, 61
GDP, 17, 18, 31, 50, 53, 55, 81, 82
Generally Accepted Accounting Principles, 20
geological, 6
Georgia, 101

geothermal power, 87
Germany, 25, 28, 47, 101, 107
globalization, 2
goods and services, 38
governance, 46, 69
government expenditure, 77
government procurement, 38
government securities, 18, 43
governments, vii, 2, 4, 79, 83, 100
governor, 48
GPA, 100
grandfathered, 32
grants, 38, 64, 65, 78, 93, 94
Greece, 25, 101
gross domestic product, 17, 31, 43
growth, 17, 18, 31, 55, 75, 83, 84, 94
Guatemala, 25
guidance, 22, 27, 86
guidelines, 12, 16, 86, 89, 94
guilty, 68

H

harmonizing, 2
health, 27, 32, 60, 69, 84, 87, 88, 98
health care, 87, 88
health care system, 88
health services, 32
hedging, 99
high school, 103
higher education, 32, 102
high-priority, 37
hiring, 27
history, 76
holding company, 8
Honduras, 25
host, 78, 91
hotels, 45, 65, 78
hourly wage, 27
hub, 78
human, 23, 44, 48, 75
human resources, 48
human right, 44
human rights, 44
Hungary, 47, 101
hydrocarbons, 3, 19

I

Iceland, 25
IMF, 86
immunity, 105
implementation, 18, 25, 34, 38, 49, 60, 65, 89
import substitution, 93
imports, 5, 19, 39, 79
imprisonment, 46, 97, 101
improvements, 16, 57, 65, 69, 90
income, 16, 34, 37, 47, 49, 55, 82, 94, 98, 105
income tax, 16, 37, 47, 49, 105
increased access, 31
increased competition, 9, 17
India, 3, 25, 27, 47, 101
individuals, 73, 75, 89, 95
Indonesia, 1, iii, v, 31, 32, 33, 34, 35, 36, 37, 38, 39, 40, 41, 42, 43, 44, 45, 46, 47, 48, 49, 50, 51, 52, 67, 101
Indonesian, 31, 32, 35, 36, 37, 38, 39, 40, 41, 42, 43, 44, 45, 46, 48, 49
industrial relations, 104
industrial sectors, 58, 84
industries, 4, 11, 12, 32, 43, 47, 56, 67, 103
industry, 2, 6, 7, 11, 12, 19, 27, 48, 50, 65, 69, 71, 72, 85, 88, 89, 103, 104, 106
inflation, 17, 74, 82
inflexible, 55, 57
information exchange, 25
information technology, 81, 84
infrastructure, 7, 9, 11, 19, 20, 31, 33, 35, 44, 64, 74, 78, 83, 84, 87, 94
initiation, 97
injuries, 45, 69
inspections, 69, 88, 98

inspectors, 98
institutions, 8, 17, 18, 23, 32, 43, 72, 86
integration, 12, 89
intellectual property, 14, 15, 37, 40, 57, 65, 82, 96, 97
intellectual property rights, 14, 37, 40, 57, 65, 96
interest groups, 57
interest rates, 17, 34, 74, 93
interference, 44, 99, 100
internal controls, 46
Internal Revenue Service, 25
international arena, 82
international law, 10, 62
international standards, 22, 24, 70
international trade, 2, 84
interoperability, 7
investment, vii, 2, 3, 4, 9, 10, 15, 16, 17, 18, 19, 25, 26, 32, 34, 35, 36, 37, 42, 44, 46, 47, 48, 49, 55, 56, 57, 58, 60, 62, 63, 69, 77, 78, 79, 81, 82, 83, 85, 86, 87, 88, 89, 91, 92, 93, 95, 98, 99, 101, 106
investment bank, 98
investment incentive, 55, 81, 92, 93
investments, 2, 4, 10, 11, 23, 32, 44, 45, 49, 57, 60, 62, 64, 65, 72, 75, 76, 77, 78, 81, 89, 92, 93, 101, 102
investors, vii, 1, 2, 4, 5, 6, 8, 9, 10, 11, 18, 31, 32, 34, 35, 36, 37, 39, 41, 42, 45, 47, 48, 49, 56, 57, 58, 60, 63, 64, 65, 69, 70, 71, 72, 73, 74, 76, 78, 79, 84, 85, 86, 88, 90, 91, 92, 93, 95, 99, 102
ions, 24
IPR, 14, 15, 40, 65, 67, 96, 97
Iran, 47, 101
Iraq, 100
iron, 39, 85
Israel, 101
issues, 2, 4, 25, 36, 49, 68, 71, 75, 77, 82, 83, 86, 88, 92, 96
Italy, 25, 47, 101, 107
iteration, 32

J

Jamaica, 47
Japan, 25, 28, 47, 50, 51, 52, 56, 79, 101
Java, 52
job creation, 23
Jordan, 47, 101
judicial, 7, 11, 23, 36, 85, 89, 92, 96, 100
judiciary, 76, 90, 92
jurisdiction, 26, 36

K

Kazakhstan, 102
kidnapping, 100
knowledge-based economy, 86
Korea, v, 47, 50, 51, 55, 56, 57, 58, 60, 63, 64, 65, 66, 67, 68, 69, 70, 71, 72, 73, 74, 75, 76, 77, 78, 79
Kurds, 100
Kuwait, 102
Kyrgyzstan, 47, 102

L

labor force, 102
labor market, 26, 41, 55, 72, 85
labor markets, 55
laboratory studies, 94
lamented, 31
land acquisition, 35, 36, 40, 41
languages, 69
Laos, 47
largest markets, 1
Latin America, 22
Latvia, 102
law enforcement, 23, 45, 46, 66, 96
laws, vii, 10, 14, 17, 24, 25, 31, 36, 40, 41, 46, 48, 64, 70, 71, 76, 92, 97, 98
laws and regulations, 41, 71
lawyers, 10, 37, 63
lead, 35, 100

Lebanon, 102
LEED, 78
legislation, 9, 24, 26, 36, 45, 72, 85, 98, 100, 104
legitimate, 90
lending, 8, 17, 18, 70, 72, 73, 102
liberalization, 62
licenses, 32, 33, 35, 49, 87
light, 87
limited liability, 14
liquidation, 34, 43
liquidity, 42, 56, 74
Lithuania, 102
litigation, 35, 63, 97
livestock, 39, 67
loans, 9, 18, 42, 47, 94, 98, 102, 106
local government, 19, 32, 33, 40, 45, 58, 78, 85
logistics, 56, 78
lower prices, 9

M

Macedonia, 102
machinery, 37, 49, 85, 93
macroeconomic policy, 31
magazines, 59
majority, 7, 35, 56, 73, 74, 101
Malaysia, 25, 47, 50, 51, 102
management, 22, 23, 27, 37, 41, 44, 57, 60, 65, 71, 73, 75, 82, 99, 103
manipulation, 70
manpower, 37
manufacturing, 2, 27, 55, 64, 67, 78, 85, 103, 105, 106
market access, 47
market capitalization, 73, 99
market concentration, 4
market share, 17, 43, 75
marketing, 5, 19, 32, 89, 97
mass, 22
material sciences, 83
materials, 3, 66, 69
Mauritius, 47
maximum, 13, 14, 17, 38, 46, 49, 88
maximum price, 88
meat, 59
mechanism, 2, 57
mediation, 14, 39, 48, 103
medical, 76, 85, 89
membership, 9, 103, 105
merchandise, 27
mergers, 43, 56, 65, 73
metals, 24, 60
metropolitan areas, 22
Mexico, 1, iii, v, 1, 2, 3, 4, 5, 6, 7, 8, 9, 10, 11, 12, 13, 14, 15, 16, 18, 19, 20, 21, 22, 23, 24, 25, 26, 27, 28, 47
middle class, 31
Middle East, 42, 45, 82, 107
military, 44, 72, 76, 94, 100, 104
minimum wage, 27, 48, 68
mining, 32, 33, 35, 36, 43, 49, 95
Ministry of Education, 103
minors, 68
misuse, 35
models, 9
modernizing, vii, 70
modifications, 12
modules, 69
Moldova, 102
monetary limits, 10
monetary policy, 18
money laundering, 9, 24, 26, 41, 61
Mongolia, 47, 102
monopoly, 19, 21
moral hazard, 72
Morocco, 47, 102
Mozambique, 47
Multilateral, 47, 64, 77
multinational companies, 86
multinational firms, 45
municipal power, 5
music, 66, 96

N

NAFTA, 3, 4, 8, 9, 10, 11, 12, 15, 18, 25
narcotics, 22
national security, 4, 60, 72
nationalism, 35
nationality, 85, 90
NATO, 99
natural gas, 5, 6, 19, 104
natural gas pipeline, 6
natural hazards, 83
natural resources, 33, 40
negotiating, 47, 101
negotiation, 39
Netherlands, 25, 47, 56, 102, 107
neutral, 19, 27, 63
new media, 7
New York Stock Exchange, 6
New Zealand, 47
NGOs, 86
Nicaragua, 25
non-domestic, 90
North America, 3, 78
North American Free Trade Agreement, 3
North Korea, 47, 66, 76
Northeast Asia, 78
Norway, 47
notary, 39
nuisance, 49

O

OAS, 24
obstacles, 14, 48
OECD, 4, 9, 16, 22, 24, 26, 27, 44, 46, 58, 62, 67, 68, 71, 76, 90, 100
officials, 16, 24, 31, 45, 67, 71, 75, 89, 100, 101
oil, 5, 19, 21, 32, 33, 35, 39, 49, 91, 104
old age, 48
opaque, 57
open economy, 4
operations, 2, 4, 6, 8, 19, 20, 23, 24, 26, 27, 34, 35, 41, 42, 43, 44, 45, 95, 100
opportunities, 41, 85, 88, 92, 99
ores, 39
Organization for Economic Cooperation and Development, 90
organize, 67
organized labor, 67
outsourcing, 27, 41, 48
overlap, 33
overseas investment, 75
Overseas Private Investment Corporation, 26, 47, 77, 102
oversight, 23, 24
overtime, 68, 69
ownership, 5, 6, 8, 9, 13, 32, 36, 40, 43, 49, 60, 65, 69, 70, 71, 73, 76

P

Pacific, 2, 6, 76
Pakistan, 47, 102
palm oil, 39
PAN, 1
Panama, 25
parallel, 71, 89
parents, 68
Parliament, 41, 85, 92, 96, 100, 101, 103
patents, 15
payroll, 11
peace, 61, 76
penalties, 14, 24, 76, 96, 97
per capita income, 93
permission, 7, 64, 68, 93, 95
permit, 2, 4, 19, 20, 38, 62, 71, 76, 89, 97
persons with disabilities, 68
Peru, 2, 25, 47
petroleum, 3, 4, 5, 6, 19, 91, 95
Petroleum, 3, 5, 19, 91
pharmaceutical, 85, 88, 89, 96
pharmaceuticals, 97
Philippines, 47, 67, 102
physical, 34, 40, 81, 84

pipeline, 6, 97
piracy, 14, 40, 65, 66, 67, 96, 97
plants, 20, 64
platform, 5, 46, 86
playing, 41, 56, 70
pluralism, 67
Poland, 47, 102
police, 45, 76, 99, 100, 104
policy, 15, 18, 57, 69, 72, 73, 75, 84, 89
policy issues, 84
policy makers, 57, 69
political parties, 1, 44
population, 17, 67, 76, 88, 102
portability, 7
portfolio, 43, 56, 73, 84
portfolio investment, 43, 56, 84
Portugal, 25, 102
postal service, 21
power generation, 3, 19, 59, 60
power plants, 87
precedent, 36
predictability, 82, 89
pregnancy, 27
preparation, 64
presidency, 9
president, 1, 24
President, 1, 4, 5, 9, 13, 15, 20, 21, 23, 26, 44, 45, 46, 56, 75, 77, 83
President Clinton, 77
President Obama, 83
primary school, 102
principles, 62, 71
private enterprises, 95
private firms, 6, 19
private investment, 6, 19, 102
private ownership, 39, 40, 64
private sector, 2, 16, 17, 71, 85, 86, 87, 99, 102
privatization, 21, 43, 73, 85
probe, 100
procurement, 16, 38, 60, 94, 98, 100
procurements, 38
producers, 5, 12, 20, 35, 105
product design, 94
productivity, 4, 19, 85
professionalism, 70
profit, 23, 34, 43
project, 34, 60, 78, 87, 89, 103
property rights, 35, 37, 95
protection, 14, 23, 25, 35, 40, 46, 47, 65, 66, 92, 96, 97, 98, 101
prototype, 94
provision, 9, 91
public administration, 24
public awareness, 96, 97
public corporations, 60
public enterprises, 95
public officials, 46
public sector, 22, 61, 65, 98
public-private partnerships, 83
publishing, 89
punishment, 97, 101
PVP, 97

Q

quality of life, 79

R

radio, 3
radioactive waste, 60
ratification, 15, 96
raw materials, 12, 49, 81
real estate, 2, 8, 11, 56, 65, 74, 95, 106
real property, 55, 65, 91, 95
reality, 36, 43
reciprocity, 6
recommendations, 66, 71, 86
recreational, 78
reform, 1, 5, 11, 17, 19, 20, 23, 26, 41, 70, 86, 88, 92
Reform, 32
reforms, 5, 16, 18, 21, 41, 72, 82, 86, 89, 96, 100

registries, 14
regulations, 5, 13, 15, 16, 19, 20, 31, 33, 34, 37, 38, 41, 49, 57, 58, 65, 68, 69, 70, 71, 73, 82, 85, 87, 93, 97, 103, 105
regulatory agencies, 15, 56
regulatory bodies, 7
regulatory changes, 41, 72
regulatory framework, 48
regulatory requirements, 95
reinsurance, 47
related ministries, 32
relaxation, 73
relief, 17, 88
renewable energy, 5, 87, 102
rent, 41, 64
repair, 27
repatriate, 34
repatriation, 34, 73, 91
repo, 90
reputation, 56, 102
require, 4, 5, 10, 21, 27, 32, 34, 36, 41, 42, 46, 60, 66, 68, 73, 75, 81, 87
requirements, 2, 3, 4, 7, 10, 11, 17, 22, 25, 33, 37, 38, 40, 60, 64, 65, 70, 79, 89, 93
researchers, 83, 94
reserves, 5, 73
resistance, 20
resolution, 48
resource management, 75
resources, 2, 20, 33, 37
response, 45, 69, 71
restriction, 39
restrictions, 3, 4, 8, 26, 31, 34, 41, 47, 48, 62, 65, 73, 91, 98, 104, 105
restructuring, 65
retail, 19, 40, 74, 78
retained earnings, 18, 50
retirement, 48, 77
revenue, 18, 21, 39
rights, 8, 10, 14, 19, 35, 37, 40, 63, 64, 65, 67, 68, 70, 71, 92, 93, 96, 104
risk, 26, 72, 99, 102
risk assessment, 72
risks, vii, 9, 56
Romania, 47, 102
routes, 22, 100
royalties, 9, 34, 36, 62, 91
royalty, 35
rubber, 39
rule of law, 23
rules, 2, 13, 14, 21, 36, 37, 41, 63, 71, 75, 82, 84
rules of origin, 2
rural areas, 45
rural population, 82
Russia, 3, 25

S

safeguards, 35
safety, 69, 98
sanctions, 24
Sarbanes-Oxley Act, 70
Saudi Arabia, 25, 47, 102
savings, 90
school, 68, 78, 79, 87, 102, 103
schooling, 102
science, 44, 83
SCT, 8
securities, 18, 19, 34, 43, 62, 99
securities firms, 18
security, 23, 32, 35, 45, 60, 83, 95, 99, 100, 101
security forces, 45, 100
security guard, 99
security services, 32
seed, 97
seizure, 97
sell the airline, 8
sellers, 74
Senate, 9, 10
sentiment, 55
September 11, 100
Serbia, 102
servers, 66

service provider, 66, 76
services, 2, 3, 4, 6, 7, 14, 18, 21, 26, 32, 40, 45, 60, 69, 76, 82, 84, 93
sex, 27
shareholders, 13, 14, 35, 42, 56, 70, 71, 73, 93, 95, 105
Sharia, 42
shortage, 27, 103
Singapore, 25, 47, 49, 50, 51, 102
six notches, 84
skilled workers, 27, 48
Slovakia, 25, 102
social responsibility, 21, 22, 75
social safety nets, 23
social security, 40, 105
Social Security, 48, 88
social welfare, 56
society, 23, 55
software, 40, 65, 66, 67, 94, 96
South Africa, 47
South America, 106, 107
South Korea, 1, iii, v, 25, 47, 55, 56, 57, 58, 60, 61, 62, 63, 64, 67, 70, 73, 74, 75, 76, 77, 102
soybean, 39
Spain, 7, 25, 28, 47, 102
specialists, 83
speculation, 35
spending, 56, 88
spot market, 87
Sri Lanka, 47
stability, 1, 73, 76
standardization, 105
state, 2, 4, 5, 9, 10, 11, 19, 20, 21, 22, 23, 24, 32, 38, 39, 46, 57, 60, 64, 65, 74, 76, 78, 85, 88, 91, 92, 100, 101, 104
state authorities, 20
state-owned enterprises, 74
states, 2, 5, 11, 16, 24, 37, 40
statistics, 49, 66, 69
statutes, 26
steel, 39, 85
still-valid, 35
stimulus, 98
stock, 13, 14, 18, 32, 42, 43, 56, 62, 65, 70, 73, 99
stock exchange, 32, 42, 43, 70, 99
stock markets, 73
stockholders, 70
storage, 5, 19, 66, 105
strengthen, 4, 18, 23, 46, 55, 98
structural reforms, 85, 86
structure, 13, 44
subscribers, 43
subsidized, 20, 38, 93
Sudan, 47
suicide, 99
supervision, 3, 18, 72, 73
suppliers, 18, 38, 70
supply chain, 56
Supreme Court, 7, 36, 97, 101
surplus, 27
surrounding, 2, 76
surveillance, 3, 23
Sweden, 25, 47, 102
Switzerland, 15, 25, 28, 47, 102
Syria, 47, 102

T

tactics, 100
Tajikistan, 102
takeover, 99
tanks, 16
target, 81, 82
tariff, 13, 39, 47, 58, 87
Task Force, 77
tax base, 91
tax breaks, 78
tax collection, 90
tax evasion, 25
tax holiday, 37
tax incentive, 11, 37, 58, 60
tax rates, 90
tax reform, 90
tax reforms, 90

taxation, 25, 44, 90
taxes, 11, 25, 26, 62, 85, 90, 94, 105
taxpayers, 105
teachers, 100, 104
technical assistance, 23, 69
techniques, 23
technologies, 83
technology, 27, 37, 55, 58, 60, 62, 64, 74, 81, 85, 88, 93, 94, 96
technology transfer, 60, 81, 93, 94
telecommunications, 4, 6, 7, 37, 43, 59, 60
Telecommunications Act, 66
telephone, 59
tension, 76
tensions, 76
tenure, 77
terminals, 6
territory, 8
terrorism, 45
terrorist groups, 100
terrorist organization, 45
terrorists, 45
test data, 96
textiles, 39, 106
Thailand, 47, 102
threats, 45, 76
time deposits, 90
time-consuming, 63
tobacco, 106
torture, 23
total energy, 43
tourism, 3, 43
toys, 39
TPI, 96
trade, 1, 2, 4, 12, 27, 47, 68, 82, 83, 84, 88, 97, 103, 104
trade deficit, 82
trade policy, 12
trade union, 68, 103, 104
trademarks, 65
trafficking, 23
training, 4, 11, 23, 37, 69, 97, 103
training programs, 11, 37, 103
transactions, 2, 4, 5, 9, 11, 16, 26, 34, 61, 62, 74, 90
translation, 63
transmission, 3, 19
transparency, 16, 25, 41, 46, 57, 61, 72, 82, 89, 97, 98, 101
transport, 9, 59, 106
transportation, 3, 4, 5, 6, 19, 60, 87, 95, 104
Treasury, 39, 42, 86, 93
Treasury bills, 42
treaties, 15, 25, 41
treatment, 3, 4, 10, 18, 37, 38, 93
Trinidad, 25
Trinidad and Tobago, 25
Turkey, 1, iii, v, 47, 81, 82, 83, 84, 85, 86, 87, 88, 89, 91, 92, 93, 94, 95, 96, 97, 98, 99, 100, 101, 102, 104, 105, 106, 107
Turkish republic, 81
Turkmenistan, 47, 102
turnover, 73

U

U.S. and Canada, 8, 18
U.S. Department of Commerce, 82
Ukraine, 47, 102
UN, 36, 44, 46, 68, 78, 101
uncertainty, 33, 41, 55, 57
unemployment rate, 67, 102
unions, 27, 67, 68, 74, 103, 104
United, 2, 9, 10, 11, 15, 18, 20, 22, 23, 24, 25, 28, 46, 47, 56, 63, 76, 77, 79, 82, 83, 84, 91, 96, 99, 101, 102
United Kingdom, 25, 28, 46, 47, 102
United Nations, 10, 22, 24, 63, 76, 77, 84
United States, 2, 9, 11, 15, 18, 23, 25, 28, 47, 56, 63, 77, 79, 82, 83, 91, 96, 99, 101, 102
universities, 65, 103
unprocessed, 39

updating, 58
urban, 82, 100, 102, 104
urban areas, 100, 102
Uruguay, 25
usually levied, 63
Uzbekistan, 47, 102

V

valuation, 35, 62
value-added goods, 84
VAT, 40, 49, 93, 94
vehicles, 100
venture capital, 99
veto, 27
victims, 100
Vietnam, 47, 67
violence, 22, 23, 76
volatility, 57, 74
vote, 101
voting, 18

W

wages, 48, 67, 69, 94
war, 47, 76
Washington, 83
waste, 60
water, 19, 20, 59, 75, 104
water resources, 75
wealth, 33, 44, 75
web, 71, 93
web sites, 71
welfare, 90
wells, 5
wholesale, 5, 7
wind power, 87
wireless, 6, 7
wood, 39
worker rights, 77
workers, 27, 37, 40, 45, 48, 67, 68, 69, 85, 103, 104
workforce, 57, 68, 69, 84, 102, 103
working groups, 83
workplace, 67
World Bank, 3, 16, 29, 33, 47, 61, 64, 77, 82, 86, 89, 90
World Trade Organization, 64
worldwide, 106
WTO, 7, 15, 37, 60, 64, 92, 98, 100

Y

Yemen, 47, 102
youth unemployment, 102

Z

Zimbabwe, 47